"Simon Harak's passion for companionship with Jesus infused his constant search for nonviolent ways to resist war and cruelty. Simon opened doors for his friends, students, and loved ones to deepen their relationship to Jesus and the Gospels. Philip, his brother, readily joined the journey. Their meditations reveal the beautiful life of a man who was uproariously funny, constantly kind, and lovingly courageous. *Living in the Company of Jesus* invites readers to follow Simon's lead."

—KATHY KELLY, president, World BEYOND War

"*Living in the Company of Jesus* is already creating the me I pray to be here, now, and forever. For thirty years I'd already learned much from my friends Simon and Phil Harak. In print, their wisdom leaps off the page. I dwell in it. Martin Luther King Jr. taught me long ago that gospel nonviolence is a 'way of life.' Their book helps me live it."

—SR. JANE MORRISSEY, SSJ, co-author of *Gracias, Matiox, Thanks, Hermano Pedro: A Trilingual Anthology of Guatemalan Oral Tradition*

"A powerful and compelling exploration of the Gospels through the lens of nonviolence—the mystery of love confronting the mystery of evil—engaging the imagination, intellect, and heart. Written with clarity, passion, and a sense of urgency, it challenges both those deeply grounded and those new to the story of Jesus in the New Testament Scriptures to see with new eyes their encounter and relationship with themselves, others, creation, and the sacred."

—THOMAS DAVID MCMURRAY, SJ, chaplain and director of Mission and Identity, Nativity School of Worcester

"A profound gift of luminous insight, *Living in the Company of Jesus* draws us into a rich study of Jesus' nonviolent love and liberation and its application to our everyday lives. Combining their shared scholarly expertise, spiritual insights, and deeply rooted commitment to social justice, the Harak brothers help us see that Jesus, his life experiences, and Christian discipleship are not simply concepts beyond our reach, but are truly present and possible here and now."

—CAROL M. LUKENS, educator and nonviolence advocate

Living in the Company of Jesus

Living in the Company of Jesus

A Practical, Scripture-Based Guide to Deepening Your
Journey within His Nonviolent Kingdom

Philip J. Harak
G. Simon Harak, SJ

FOREWORD BY
Reverend Emmanuel Charles McCarthy

CASCADE *Books* · Eugene, Oregon

LIVING IN THE COMPANY OF JESUS
A Practical, Scripture-Based Guide to Deepening Your Journey within His Nonviolent Kingdom

Cascade Books
An Imprint of Wipf and Stock Publishers
199 W. 8th Ave., Suite 3
Eugene, OR 97401

www.wipfandstock.com

PAPERBACK ISBN: 978-1-6667-3773-8
HARDCOVER ISBN: 978-1-6667-9750-3
EBOOK ISBN: 978-1-6667-9751-0

Cataloguing-in-Publication data:

Names: Harak, Philip J., author. | Harak, G. Simon, author. | McCarthy, Emmanuel Charles, foreword.

Title: Living in the company of Jesus : a practical, Scripture-based guide to deepening your journey within his nonviolent kingdom / Philip J. Harak and G. Simon Harak; foreword by Emmanuel Charles McCarthy.

Description: Eugene, OR: Cascade Books, 2022 | Includes bibliographical references.

Identifiers: ISBN 978-1-6667-3773-8 (paperback) | ISBN 978-1-6667-9750-3 (hardcover) | ISBN 978-1-6667-9751-0 (ebook)

Subjects: LCSH: Jesus Christ—Teachings | Nonviolence—Religious aspects—Christianity. | Pacifism—Religious aspects—Christianity.

Classification: BT736.6 L40 2022 (print) | BT736.6 (ebook)

To Simon, Brother in Blood, Brother in Christ, Brother in the Kingdom, Embraced for Eternity as a Child of God

Jesus proclaimed, "The kingdom of heaven is at hand. Repent, and believe in the gospel."

MARK 1:15

Table of Contents

Foreword by Reverend Emmanuel Charles McCarthy xiii
Preface xix
Acknowledgments xxv
List of Abbreviations xxvii
Introduction xxix

Chapter 1: Mary's Immaculate Conception Presents
to All Believers God's Liberating Graces 1

    The Immaculate Conception
    Philip's Reflection
    Questions to Consider

Chapter 2: Why Was Joseph Afraid? (Matt 1:18–25) 7

    Breaking the Patriarchy
    Philip's Reflection
    Questions to Consider

Chapter 3: Jesus Saves Peter and Us on Turbulent Waters
(Matt 14:22–33) 11

    Peter on the Water
    Philip's Reflection
    Questions to Consider

Chapter 4: Jesus Faithfully Searches for All to Return
to the Kingdom (Luke 15:1–11) 16

    The Lost Sheep and the Lost Coin
    Philip's Reflection
    Questions to Consider

Chapter 5: Sharing the Christ-Life within Us (Luke 2:1–20) 22

A Midnight Mass Reflection
Philip's Reflection
Questions to Consider

Chapter 6: Whom Do We Hear When Jesus Calls the Twelve Disciples?
(Matt 4: 18–22; Mark 1:16–20, 2:13–17; Luke 5:1–11, 27–33;
John 1:35–51) 27

The Calling of the Twelve Disciples
Philip's Reflection
Questions to Consider

Chapter 7: Jesus' Nonviolent Direct Action in the Temple
(Luke 19:28–49 and 21:1–4) 33

Widows
Philip's Reflection
Questions to Consider

Chapter 8: Why Did the Congregation Want to Kill Jesus after Hearing
His First Sermon? (Luke 4:16–30) 39

Jesus' First Sermon
Philip's Reflection
Questions to Consider

Chapter 9: What We Learn from the Syrophoenician Woman's Great Faith
(Matt 15:21–29) 47

The Syrophoenician Woman
Philip's Reflection
Questions to Consider

Chapter 10: Jesus' Incarnation Heals Us and Empowers Us to Ministry
(Mark 7:31–37) 54

On Jesus' Healing in the Decapolis
Philip's Reflection
Questions to Consider

Chapter 11: How We Can Return to God's Kingdom (Matt 13:31–33) 59

The Mustard Seed and the Yeast
Philip's Reflection
Questions to Consider

Chapter 12: All Live Life in Its Fullness in God's Kingdom
(Matt 20:1–17) 64

The Workers in the Vineyard
Philip's Reflection
Questions to Consider

Chapter 13: How Friends of Jesus Grieve Dying and Death
(John 11:1–44) 70

Jesus and Lazarus
Philip's Reflection
Questions to Consider

Chapter 14: Who or What Provides a Christian's True Security?
(Luke 22:54–62) 77

On Peter's Betrayal of Jesus
Philip's Reflection
Questions to Consider

Chapter 15: Jesus' Nonviolent Conversion of Death:
Running with Open Hearts to His Empty Tomb (John 20:1–18) 83

The Resurrection
Philip's Reflection
Questions to Consider

Chapter 16: How Should Christian Communities Treat Internal
Dissenters? (John 20:24–30) 88

Thomas the Unbeliever
Philip's Reflection
Questions to Consider

TABLE OF CONTENTS

Chapter 17: We Enact God-Like Love When We Forgive Enemies
and Friends (John 21:1–20) 96

Forgiving Peter
Philip's Reflection
Questions to Consider

Chapter 18: We Are One with Christ Jesus 102

St. Cecilia
Philip's Reflection
Questions to Consider

Chapter 19: Jesus' Call to His Beloved Cannot Be Silenced
(2 Tim 2:8–13) 109

St. Paul Miki and Companions, Martyrs
Philip's Reflection
Questions to Consider

Afterword 115

Appendix A: Best Practices Guidelines
for Individual, Pair, or Group Study 119
Appendix B: Final Review and Application Questions 125

Bibliography 127

Foreword

THERE IS AN ABUNDANCE of books resting peacefully and undisturbed on the shelves of the libraries of the world, which argue against or generate ambiguity about such issues as the nonviolence of Jesus, the divinity of Jesus, and the resurrection of Jesus. *Living in the Company of Jesus*, by Philip Harak and Simon Harak, SJ, is not one of them. *Living in the Company of Jesus* embraces wholeheartedly as a matter of faith and gospel truth that Jesus is the Word of God, "made flesh," that he is risen from the dead, and that he teaches by his words and deeds in the Gospels a way of nonviolent love of all under all circumstances.

To say that Jesus teaches a way of nonviolent love of friends and enemies and to say that Jesus is God incarnate, and to say that Jesus is risen from the dead, is to say only what the Gospels say. It is also to say what most people, and perhaps what most Christians, will not say.

Living in the Company of Jesus is a scholarly and pastorally life-giving exegesis, illumination, and exploration of what the unconditional and unequivocal acceptance of these three stupendous truths of the Gospels mean for each person chosen by Jesus to be his disciple, and for every human being who ever lived, lives, or will live. The hope lying between its covers, like an uncarved *Pieta* that lies within a block of Carrara marble, is that the thoughts therein will by the grace of God disclose that Jesus is a person of nonviolent love, is risen from the dead and is God incarnate, thereby intensifying the reader's love of and relationship with Jesus, and through him with the Father, and with all the Father's sons and daughters.

In the 1920s and 1930s, Dutch Schultz was a much feared, major league gangster in New York City. He was a brutal, big-time thug whose gang of sociopaths engaged in every manner of crime and immorality. On October 23, 1935, he was shot by order of another crime boss, Lucky

Luciano. He held onto life for a day in a hospital. On his deathbed he asked to be baptized. A priest from a local Catholic church came, and after determining that Schultz was never baptized—he was Jewish—and that he was sincere in his desire to be baptized, administered to him the sacrament of baptism and the last rites of the Church. He was buried from a Catholic church and his body was interred in Gate of Heaven Catholic Cemetery.

You would have thought that there would have been great happiness among Catholics and Christians because he, who was lost, was saved. But such was not the case. All hell broke out in the church. Catholics and Christians of other churches were enraged at the priest who baptized Dutch Schultz, and at the Church for approving of his baptism. The general refrain of their fury was that Schultz was a wicked man, who after a life of monstrous public evil, got a free ticket into heaven—a ticket that these irate Catholics and other Christians believed they had been working hard to try to get.

It is as if these Christians never heard that Jesus said, "I want mercy, not sacrifice,"[1] and "I came not to condemn the world but to save it."[2] It is as if they had never heard his teaching regarding there "being more rejoicing in heaven over one sinner who repents than over ninety-nine righteous persons who do not need to repent."[3] Or, had not listened to what Jesus said to the criminal crucified next to him who asked, "Jesus, remember me when you come into in your kingdom," and who instantly received Jesus' response, "I promise you, this day you will be with me in Paradise."[4]

Of course, Catholics and other Christians in 1935 heard or read these words of Jesus on forgiveness many times over since childhood. The issue then as now is that "their hearts had grown callous, they hear but do not understand, lest they should turn and be healed."[5] It is as Jesus said to Peter two thousand years ago: "You are thinking not as God does, but as men do,"[6] when Peter tries to convince Jesus to go along with Peter's way rather than the way Jesus has chosen because it is the will of the Father.

One of the major purposes of the incarnation and of *Living in the Company of Jesus* is to bring people to think like God thinks. The first

1. Matt 9:13.
2. John 3:17.
3. Luke 15:7.
4. Luke 23:42–43.
5. Matt 13:15; Acts 28:27.
6. Matt 16:23.

word out of Jesus' mouth in his public ministry in the Gospel of Matthew is "*metanoia*,"[7] which means change your mind, think differently, repent. "Into what should I change my mind?" a person asks. The answer is, "Put on the mind of Christ." "Why put on his mind?" is the obvious next question. The answer is that because Christ is the incarnation of God, and his mind is the mind of God "made flesh." So, if you desire to think like God thinks and love as God loves, then thinking as Jesus thinks and loving as Jesus loves is the way to fulfill that desire and enter into the life and promises that desire contains.

Living in the Company of Jesus is a sacramental piece of writing, which draws its reader into the power to think like God thinks and to love as Jesus loves—into the power to enthusiastically rejoice that Dutch Schultz is saved, as well as into the power that saved Dutch Schultz. In other words, given the chance, *Living in the Company of Jesus* will draw a Christian or anyone else into a deeper communion with the mind of God via the mind of Jesus, and thereby make available to the person, in his or her own unique life, the motivation and power to conform his or her deeds, moment to moment, with loving as Christ-God loves.

Since Jesus knows that God is Father, that God is love, he also knows what is not love, what is not of God, and what never can be the will of the Father on earth or in heaven, and so also will those who put on the mind of Christ and think like God thinks. As is made so clear chapter after chapter in *Living in the Company of Jesus*, Jesus rejects violence and enmity, retaliation and greed, dominative power and indifference towards relievable human suffering—values and acts that most of humanity emphatically embraces. This rejection is not ultimately the consequence of following some law of man or God, but of living in, by, and through the mind of God who is love and the Father of all, who wants none of his sons or daughters to be agents of, or subjected to, the evils of violence and enmity, retaliation and greed, dominative power, and indifference towards relievable human suffering. What father or mother would? What father or mother would not want their children to think as they think on this matter? As God thinks?

That being so, to love as our Father, our Mother, loves is to live according to the image and likeness of God, in whose image and likeness we are all created.[8] To live in the image and likeness of our Father, our Mother, is to be fully human—which is not the same as being fully American,

---

7. Matt 4:17.

8. See Gen 1:26–27.

Russian, Chinese, English, French, etc. "We have put on a new self, which is being renewed in knowledge in the image of the Creator. Here there is no Greek or Jew, barbarian or Scythian, slave or free but Christ is all and in all. Therefore clothe yourselves with hearts of compassion, kindness, humility, gentleness and patience."[9]

Jesus is "the visible image of the invisible God."[10] He is the "image and likeness" of God as completely as it can be known on this earth. He is the "eldest" Son in the Father's human family, who is the model for all his siblings. But, Jesus is not a dead brother whom we try to imitate solely by reading his words, looking at his picture, or poring over biographies about him. Jesus is risen from the dead. He is alive and well and active. He is "Emmanuel, God with us"[11] during our time on earth and beyond. He is present and loving us whether or not we pay any attention to him or call upon him. He is present at every instant of each life and is ever open to a momentary or to a prolonged brotherly relationship.

The primary purpose for *Living in the Company of Jesus* is that its reader should have and grow in a personal relationship with Jesus in order to know, love, and serve the Father and his sons and daughters in this world, and be in eternal communion with the Father and with all the reader's brothers and sisters in the family of the Father of all in the next. There is, however, a second objective that Philip and Simon Harak hope to accomplish. That objective is to expose people to the practices and characteristics of Ignatian spirituality as a means for fostering the primary purpose of this book. The motivation to include this as a facet of the book, I am sure, arises from how much both have received in their lives by choosing this manner of encountering God and discerning his will.

God who *is love,* who is *Father,* is of infinite depth. Therefore, the Gospels are of infinite depth because the Gospels are at their root about God. There is no limit on what Jesus through the Gospels can communicate to each and every person in his or her particular situation in life, if he or she is attentive. Hence, the Gospels, while being two thousand years old, are ever new in the strictest sense of the word "new." Perhaps therein lies the spiritual "utility" of the Ignatian spiritual process, which is a way of our honing and persevering in attentiveness to the ever-present Jesus and to the application of his mind and heart to the events of our daily life.

9. Col 3:10–13.

10. Col 1:15.

11. Matt 1:23.

Living in the Company of Jesus goes to the heart of the matter for which each Christian and indeed each person pines—even Dutch Schultz and those "thinking not as God does, but as men do,"[12] who wanted him condemned. The heart of the matter goes to the fulfillment of the divinely embedded desire, indeed longing, to consciously live in the company of God who is love, who loves each by name, and from whose love nothing in time or in eternity can separate us.

—Reverend Emmanuel Charles McCarthy

12. Matt 16:23.

Preface

I GLANCED AROUND THE large, plain room filled with about one hundred seated men, women, and children who looked battered by life. Adjusting again on the cold metal folding chair, I waited with them for Easter Sunday morning Mass to begin. I knew that the Jesuit priest celebrant would teach with passion and full certainty something about the Scriptures and the resurrection that would help me, and us, to *know* that Christ had risen and was among us now. I was sure because the man was my older brother. I had felt and witnessed the galvanizing effects his compelling talks about Jesus and his kingdom of nonviolent peace and justice had on me, churchgoers, his college students, his audience at public lectures, his fellow priests, and on his family and many friends worldwide.

In that homeless shelter in 1993 in Bridgeport, Connecticut, my brother in Christ, G. Simon Harak, started the Mass by telling us all something I recall with hope today, especially when I grieve the death of loved ones. There was an order of priests in the Middle East that traced its origins back to St. Paul.[1] Prior to each Easter Mass at dawn, all the priests in the community gathered in a space behind the altar. Shielded from the congregation's view, those priests would laugh heartily for about a minute. Imagine, Simon said, only hearing from the altar laughter, symbolizing the joy of the angels, because at times we may not *see* Christ's victory, just as we could not see those laughing. But on this day, we joyfully celebrate that Jesus defeated death for all of us. Then Simon told us to join him in victorious laughter! While I forced a few chuckles, I looked around again, and saw many others smiling and a few children giggling. After the Mass, my brother and I joined staff and other volunteers in feeding the congregation, and many others who streamed in from the street. As we plated food in the

1. I cannot recall the order; possibly the Melchites or Maronites.

kitchen, Simon laughed again, and with great joy said, "Hey, Phil, this must have been how it felt when Jesus' disciples were feeding the five thousand!" and that time I laughed easily. Such laughter over seemingly impossible life conditions, even at death, signals victory and joy in the boundless love and omnipotence of our Lord. We were all stepping into the kingdom of God.

Today, more than two years after Simon's death, by God's grace and my brother's intercession, I can smile and laugh when I imagine him now rejoicing with the Trinity and the angels and saints.

Simon nurtured a deep companionship with the risen, nonviolent, and loving Christ. His passionate, tireless ministry impelled him to implore people to listen for Jesus' constant invitation to accompaniment, friendship, comfort, and healing. A popular spiritual director, Simon was thrilled when he guided retreatants to a deeper relationship with Jesus. Many told him (and me) that his interpretation of the Scriptures renewed their faith. He helped bring Jesus to the real parts of life, during times of pain and challenge, as well as joyful and celebratory times. Jesus was indeed alive, and his teachings remain completely practical and relevant.

Over the years, I and others urged Simon to publish his many inspiring scriptural meditations and reflections about discipleship and the kingdom. He finally began, collecting several from about 2003 to 2012. Sadly, in 2012, a rare form of dementia began its seven-year assault on his mind and body, prohibiting him from finishing. I received his incomplete draft while he was ill. I edited and completed the book by sharing my faith journey and critical inquiry—in the same way we had conversed about Jesus and had worked together to build God's nonviolent kingdom throughout our lives. I shared the book's progress with him. A few days before he died, I whispered to him that I had finished our book.

This book is not our first collaboration. We worked together on peace actions and professional endeavors. We protested at military manufacturing sites; I contributed a chapter on my peacemaking efforts in the high school for an anthology he edited;[2] I helped him revise his first book[3] for readability; and I consulted at his Marquette University Center for Peacemaking on best practices in teaching conflict resolution and management to students.

We live inundated with the destructive effects of past and current violence. The Bulletin of Atomic Scientists now places us at our closest ever

2. Philip Harak, "Nonviolence in the Schools."
3. Simon Harak, *Virtuous Passions.*

point to world annihilation through nuclear war, climate change, and other destructive realities.[4] Where is Jesus and his salvific ministry amidst our crises? The Catholic Church, through Pope Francis's historic reversal of the church's justification of war and nuclear weapons deterrence, has begun its return to Jesus' original ministry of creatively and nonviolently countering evil. In 2017, the pope urged us "to make active nonviolence our way of life . . . [and for nonviolence to] become the hallmark of our decisions, our relationships and our actions, and indeed of political life in all its forms."[5] He reasserted that even possessing nuclear weapons was immoral.[6] The book in your hands revisits Jesus' ways for each person, starting with themselves, to build a peaceful world, nonviolently, creatively, and communally.

Our book also responds to the vitally important conversations Archbishop John Wester sought in his historic pastoral letter, "Living in the Light of Christ's Peace."[7] He is the first bishop to publicly break the American Catholic Church's five-year silence on Pope Francis's historic plea for all Christians to return to Jesus' way of nonviolence. Archbishop Wester asked us "to join this conversation about the urgent need for nuclear disarmament . . . to pray together, study together, dialogue together . . . [and for] all our conversations . . . [to] be respectful, rooted in prayer, [and] based in nonviolence . . . [We should] practice and study the nonviolence of Jesus daily, so that we can decrease our violence and become peacemakers."[8] Our book aids in those vital conversations by providing readers with Scripture-based truths, and many practical ways we can emulate Jesus.

We clearly present the architecture of God's kingdom based on what Jesus said and did. Our reflections remind readers that Jesus' kingdom is based on agape love for friends and all enemies; humble service to all; limitless mercy and forgiveness; creatively and nonviolently restoring dignity to the oppressed and offering opportunity to the oppressor to return to humanity; and genuinely attending and responding to relievable human suffering.

4. Mecklin, ed., "At doom's doorstep."

5. Francis, "Nonviolence," 1.

6. Francis, "Peace Memorial," 1.

7. Wester, "Living in the Light."

8. Wester, "Living in the Light," 32–34, 42. Also see "Treaty on the Prohibition," a UN treaty formally accepted in January, 2021, and currently signed by eighty-six signatories and sixty-six states parties, the first of which was the Vatican; and see "International Campaign," a highly effective organization and Nobel Peace Prize recipient.

Jesus' words, parables, and actions provide us with the wondrous incarnation of a relentlessly loving, infinitely merciful, and appealing God. I have led many groups using this book's reflections and format, and participants universally attest to its value in deepening their companionship with Jesus. The reader will explore the ways that Jesus taught to effectively heal today's suffering and rampant divisions. I use sixteen of Simon's insightful, provocative scriptural meditations and three of his studies of saintly discipleship as a springboard to reflect upon the ways I—and we—can seek to deepen faith and embolden discipleship. As a layperson with a rich background in social justice education, my role as a first responder to Simon's reflections is unique. I base my commentaries on his expert interpretations first on our shared love for Jesus, on our brotherly bond, and on my life as a teacher and social justice educator. We hope that our book helps readers deepen their personal, authentic relationship with the nonviolent Jesus, to see God in all creation, and to help build God's nonviolent kingdom.

To help with those goals, and to assist in analyzing this book's often startling contents, I relied upon my own prayerful faith journey, and my forty years as an educator for teens and adults in composing a study guide consisting of layers of questions for each chapter. In the appendices, I provide best practices guidelines for critically studying the chapters alone or in collaboration. I also provide review and application questions, designed to deepen one's critical thinking and prayerful integration and ongoing practice of faith.

I am certain that Simon is as excited as I in offering our insights and experiences about Jesus, the Trinity, discipleship, and building the nonviolent kingdom of God. Readers may come to know, or be reminded, that as we walk more closely with the Jesus of the Scriptures, and personally embrace God's limitless love and compassion, we become empowered by Christ-like love to replicate that love. We hope that this book will nurture those endeavors.

Here, briefly, are our backgrounds.

Philip J. Harak, EdD

The scriptural passages in our book refer to many of the social injustices that I studied during my doctoral work, and continue to work to redress. I combined my academic knowledge with my Christian discipleship to bring safe and inclusive learning environments into the secular public school setting. I wrote more than thirty curricula and pedagogy for

all learning abilities, including the high school's first peace studies and social justice courses, and cofounded and directed the high school's first peer
mediation program. In the classroom, we recognized each student's unique
background and contribution to the learning community. I also instructed
students in effective ways to identify and nonviolently address intra- and
interpersonal conflicts in and out of the classroom. I helped students understand what many adults did not, that nonviolence did not mean nonaction, and provided historically effective nonviolent revolutions.[9] While not
sitting in righteous judgment for those oppressed who fought violently, we
explored the growing awareness that acting violently is a choice, and not an
instinct.[10] Our classes answered Nobel Peace Prize laureate Mairead Maguire's question: "If we do not teach nonviolence in our educational systems
and in our religious institutions, how can we make that choice?"[11]

In 1991, mortified by the horrific realities of the US-led warfare and
genocidal actions against the Iraqi people, I could not find within my Catholic parish organized protests, or even widely voiced opposition against that
war. Therefore, I worked with the local American Friends group, which was
very active in peaceful opposition to the Gulf War. I led several "teach-ins"
at local universities, participated in weekly public protests, and served on
anti-war, educational panels at town meetings. Seeking broader affiliation
within my own religion, since 1992 I have served on the Massachusetts
state board of Pax Christi, the Catholic peace organization.

During Simon's long illness, I repeated the layperson's full Ignatian
Spiritual Exercises, under the expert spiritual direction of Thomas McMurray, SJ. The Exercises deepened my companionship with Jesus. Then and
today, I pray to continue to develop a disposition that I hope is more in line
with the mind of Christ, which I have the felt-sense is abundant with love,
forgiveness, and compassion. Simon and I refer often to specific Ignatius-
inspired prayerful techniques throughout this book.

G. Simon Harak, SJ, PhD

9. See Wink, *Jesus and Nonviolence*, especially chapters 1, 3, and 6, for some of the
recent historical examples; and Francis, "Nonviolence," 3–4, for additional evidence of
effective nonviolent actions.

10. I recognize that there are certain rare medical and psychological conditions
which remove one's freedom to choose, or ability to sympathize or feel remorse.

11. Maguire, "Non-Violence."

Simon was ordained a Jesuit in May of 1979. After earning a doctorate in theological ethics in 1985, he became a distinguished and award-winning full professor of religion at his alma mater, Fairfield University. He left Fairfield in 1998 to work full time as a peace activist and lecturer. A diligent researcher and gifted orator, he gave two thousand lectures against wars in person and over media, nationally and internationally. After working for several years as disarmament director with the War Resisters League, Simon was asked to develop and direct the Marquette University Center for Peace, which he did with great success until the illness stopped him in early 2013.

Simon's intellectual scope was impressive and his scholarship widely acknowledged. Expert in Greek and Latin, he contributed nuanced and perspicacious translations of the New Testament's original Greek. He added to the scholarly literature his unique insights and applications of intellectual giants like Aquinas.[12] He was also a devoted pastoral minister, dedicated to being what he called a "priest of the people." Prior to his homilies, I often saw him call to the altar all the children in the congregation. He taught them, and us, about Jesus and the kingdom in words that everyone could grasp.

After his death in November 2019, I was flooded by messages recounting his indelible impact upon his former students, parishioners, colleagues from universities and peace organizations, his Jesuit brothers, and friends.[13]

Readers may come to know, or be reminded, that as we walk more closely with the Jesus of the Scriptures, and personally embrace God's limitless love and compassion, we become empowered by Christ-like love to replicate that love. We hope that this book will nurture those endeavors.

12. Simon Harak, ed., *Aquinas and Empowerment*.

13. See Pasternak, "Another Death," and Philip Harak, "Remembering G. Simon Harak."

Acknowledgments

I AM FILLED WITH gratitude as I recall the many people who have contributed to and encouraged this book's completion. My eternal thanks to God for blessing me with Simon, my beloved brother in blood, in Christ, and in the kingdom.

Thanks to Carol Lukens, Simon's dear friend and frequent retreat co-presenter, who in faith entrusted me with his early writing, encouraging me with the words, "Because of your relationship with Simon, you will know what to do."

Thanks to Walter Smith, SJ, a former undergraduate professor of mine and the superior for a time at the marvelous health care facility where Simon spent his final years. Walter suggested ways in which I could structure the book and encouraged me to count on my own companionship with Jesus for guidance.

My local Pax Christi group members have been very supportive, and have provided valuable feedback on my facilitations of several of these chapters. My fellow members on the Massachusetts Pax Christi state board have encouraged me throughout. Special thanks to our newsletter editor Mike Moran, who provided early editorial commentary and published a few of my articles in the newsletter about this book.

I also relied on my friend Ed Duclos's technical wizardry and friendly encouragement as he guided me through predictable bumps in the word processing road.

I am very appreciative to Rodney, Matt, Emily, Heather, David, and the staff at Cascade Books. They have been exceptionally helpful, encouraging, and responsive to my queries.

Father Emmanuel Charles McCarthy's tireless, compelling, prophetic voice for Jesus' nonviolent way to the kingdom has been profoundly influential to me since I first attended his workshop thirty years ago. I am forever grateful to him, appreciative of his editorial advice on this book, and am humbled and edified by his contribution of the foreword.

Our siblings, Simon's fraternal twin, Adele, our sister Laurice, and brother John, have also encouraged me.

My deep gratitude and admiration for Jim Helling, who for many years has been a wise and trusted guide.

The Ignatian Spiritual Exercises have been a marvelous tool through which I have come to know Jesus more fully. I am grateful to the late James Skehan, SJ, who first led me through the Exercises thirty years ago. My profound gratitude, warmth, and love to Tom McMurray, SJ, who several years ago agreed to direct my second journey through the Exercises, and who still faithfully acts as my spiritual companion as we regularly meet via video calls. He is a genuinely Christ-centered apostle, whose love for the Trinity is boundless and contagious. I pray that others so moved would be as blessed to have as gifted a spiritual director and companion.

And finally, my deep love and gratitude for my wife, Margaret. She accompanied me for many of my visits to Simon during his illness. Her loving, God-centered support during his illness and passing cannot be overstated. She has provided valuable editorial advice, especially on early drafts I wrote after visiting Simon at the health care facility. In short, she encouraged me to write more about the joy and promise of Easter, rather than the pain and trials of Good Friday. She has helped keep me focused and grounded throughout this book's composition.

List of Abbreviations

Christian Community Bible, CCB.
Just War Theory, JWT

Introduction

OUR BOOK INVITES THE reader to come to know more fully Jesus of the Gospels. Many are introduced to God through parents, authorities, and cultural representations. But each Christian should answer the question he posed to his disciples in the Synoptic Gospels: Who do *you* say I am?[1] We may find that our answer differs from others' representations of Jesus. An important way to develop and nurture an authentic relationship with Jesus is for believers to immerse themselves prayerfully in the Scriptures.

A powerfully rich form of praying with the Scriptures was set forth by Saint Ignatius of Loyola, the Jesuit founder, almost five hundred years ago. In that contemplative practice, the person, calling to mind their deepest desires and bringing those to God, most often reads a passage from the New Testament in which Jesus is interacting with another or others.[2] The passage is read a second time, as the person imagines details by using each sense to create as full a picture as possible. We are then prompted to identify with a person in the scene, and notice again what we see and feel. Upon conclusion, we are encouraged to dialogue with Jesus, or another person in the scene, always paying careful attention to the movement of the mind and heart. The Exercises help us recognize God in all things in daily life, and to be responsive to God's movement in and around us.[3]

The overarching purpose of this form of prayer, I believe, is to come to know Jesus more deeply and personally. As our relationship deepens, the disciple is often moved to act in ways consistent with Jesus' ways and means

1. See Matt 16:13–16; Mark 8:29; Luke 9:18–20; emphasis added.

2. Several of the prayer sessions center around Old Testament and other New Testament readings as well.

3. There are several helpful books about the Spiritual Exercises, three of which I list in the bibliography. But it is best to be guided by an experienced director if one is moved to formally undertake the entire Exercises. See Jesuits.org for opportunities for formal direction through the Exercises.

of boundless love for everyone—perhaps especially our enemies. After his resurrection, Jesus commissioned his disciples to become *apostles,* from the Greek word meaning to "send forth." Like Jesus, Ignatius stressed the value of a Christian community, in which believers can support, verify, and sometimes challenge each other in the understanding of and service to God and others.

I suggest first reading the scriptural passages which begin the chapters, and as much as possible, following the steps of prayerfully contemplating them. I trust that if the reader keeps an open heart, our meditations and reflections will help recognize God's voice, and identify and overcome obstacles to God-like loving. One obstacle is the general lack of accurate information from our institutional churches on Jesus' command to love our enemies and to actively work with the oppressed in nonviolently resisting evil. Most Christians have not been taught that Jesus abhorred passive acceptance of evil, or that he preached and acted in creatively nonviolent ways to resist evil in a manner that sought to restore dignity to the oppressed, and offered a return to humanity for the oppressor. Walter Wink called that Jesus' revolutionary "third way" of responding to evil.[4]

Readers may uncover deep personal feelings of violent tendencies, resentments, of feeling unlovable or unforgiveable, or other resistances. Pope Francis reminds us that Jesus "taught that the true battlefield, where violence and peace meet, is the human heart . . .Whoever accepts the Good News of Jesus is able to acknowledge the violence within and be healed by God's mercy, becoming in turn an instrument of reconciliation."[5] Recognizing our obstacles is a necessary first step in liberation. If we choose to bring those and any woundedness to God, we can trust in return God's unconditional love and comfort, leading us to deeper healing and greater freedom.[6]

---

4. Wink, *Jesus and Nonviolence,* 3, 12–13. Wink asserted that prior to Jesus, humanity had been conditioned to respond to evil either with passive acceptance or violent opposition. Jesus introduced the third response, the thesis of Wink's excellent treatise. I highly recommend this scholarly yet accessible study of Christian nonviolence, as well as Wink's other works.

5. Francis, "Nonviolence," para.3.

6. See Au and Au, *God's Unconditional Love,* an excellent book that helps the reader understand the sense of unworthiness and provides Scripture-based and Ignatian spiritual strategies for healing shame. See also Rohr, *Breathing under Water,* for applying the Twelve Steps format in spiritual liberation.

There are three overarching themes in this book, with corresponding chapters for each. Chapters 1 through 6 explore specific ways in which we can deepen our relationship with Jesus, and nurture our personal sense of belonging in his nonviolent kingdom.

Chapters 7 through 17 articulate the different ways in which we can express our deepening personal relationship with Jesus through interpersonal and social situations. We examine the practical ways in which followers can deepen their active participation in the inclusive kingdom of God by understanding and redressing injustices and woundedness, as our Master did.

The final two chapters present models of Christian discipleship by two saints and martyrs. Their exemplary witness and resistance to evil provides inspiration for us, as we apply their faith to our lives and times.

I structured this as a kind of workbook, and the chapters need not be read in order. All but three chapters respond to a specific scriptural passage. Chapter titles signify their main idea, followed by the pertinent scriptural passage. I provide a brief overview, followed by Simon's title for his scriptural meditation. My reflection follows. I then pose questions exploring the chapter's key concepts and the reader's personal beliefs, and conclude with a summary sentence highlighting the chapter's contribution to the growing understanding of the kingdom of God.

I also provide tools that learners and my faith group participants have found effective in personal and group exploration. In Appendix A, I suggest best practices in using this book individually, in pairs, or in groups. In Appendix B, I pose critical thinking questions to assist in finalized reflection and ongoing application.

Two more notes. During a conversation, Simon and a fellow Jesuit scholar pointed out to me that Jesus spoke more about "the kingdom of God" than he did about his own Father. They emphasized that after his resurrection, Jesus spent forty days with his apostles, speaking often about the kingdom.[7] Our book explores specific aspects of Jesus' kingdom, and more importantly, the one he *enacts* in himself. His is a kingdom of nonviolence—one which he contrasted constantly with kingdoms of this world. Because of the importance of the word "kingdom," the reader should note that it carries three meanings in Jesus' spoken Aramaic. The first is "reign," the second is "sovereignty," where God acts as king, and the third means

7. Acts 1:3.

"kingly rule, royalty, or dignity befitting a king."[8] One can prayerfully consider which meaning applies in the different Scripture readings.

The second note concerns the Bibles referenced. We primarily used the *Catholic Study New American Bible, Revised New Testament*, and when footnoted, the *Christian Community Bible*.

My sincere prayer is that the reader will use these scriptural meditations to deepen their friendship and loving relationship with God and all of God's creation.

8. *New World Encyclopedia*, "Kingdom of God," lines 16–23. https://www.newworldencyclopedia.org/entry/Kingdom_of_God.

1

Mary's Immaculate Conception Presents to All Believers God's Liberating Graces

We use the model of Mary's faithful cooperation with God's will to explore Jesus' mission to fully liberate and unite all of humanity within God's eternal kingdom. Mary's unique relationship with God helps us understand that the new life that God incarnates is also a passionate plea for each of us to realize the ways in which God's love frees women—and everyone—from all societally imposed constraints upon our full humanity and liberation. Although she was specially blessed, Mary's complete abandonment to God provides a discipleship we can emulate. Like her, we are invited to intimately bear Jesus within us, and bring him into the world.

The Immaculate Conception[1]

The women I know do not greet the story of the Immaculate Conception with universal acclaim. Far from it, really. Portraying Mary as immaculate seems to place her far above us—separate from "us sinners, now, and at the hour of our death." In particular, the women with whom I've spoken feel

1. See The Catholic Encyclopedia, s.v. "Immaculate Conception," https://www.newadvent.org/cathen/07674d.htm. There is no scriptural proof of the dogma of Mary's Immaculate Conception, instituted in 1854 by Pope Pius IX. There are scriptural illustrations, such as in Gen 3:15, and Luke 1:28.

1

that they can never "measure up" to such an ideal version of Mary. They're always feeling "not good enough," "not pure enough," or "not holy enough." Add to that subjective sense of oppression the objective reality that, alone among the Christian communities, the Catholic and Orthodox Churches exclude women from official ministerial positions. Add to that the objective reality that, alone among the Christian communities, the Western Roman Catholic Church requires celibacy of its clergy, with the inevitable psychological accompaniment of considering women as temptations—unless they somehow manage to be as pure as the immaculate Mary. Put all that together and the task of communicating the good news of the Immaculate Conception becomes pretty difficult.

For me, there's a further, theological difficulty: if we consider Mary to be somehow separate from us, from us men and especially from us women, and worse, if we put her up on a pedestal, we simply lose a true theological understanding of the mission of Mary's son Jesus. Jesus came down from heaven to be one of us, to unite everyone, both Jew and Greek, both male and female, together in one body, "for through him we both have access in one Spirit to the Father."[2] If I hold to that understanding of his mission, it simply cannot be true that he who became one of us would want his mother to be set apart from us. Additionally, the strategy of separation is almost always the strategy of dehumanization, domination, and, eventually, the strategy of violence.

So how might I consider this feast to be life-giving, as the good news of peace? Let's start with the basics. Let's start with the poor. Specifically, let's start with a peasant girl named Bernadette of Soubirous, in France. I remember this story of Bernadette from reading Franz Werfel's book *Song of Bernadette*.

Everyone in the town, especially the church authorities, were appropriately skeptical about this impoverished daughter of a miller, and her visions of a "most, most beautiful lady"[3] with a rose on each foot, and about the mystical conversation held between these two peasant women. Prompted to discover the lady's name, Bernadette finally heard the lady say words she had to rehearse several times to remember: "I am the Immaculate Conception."[4] Under the withering interrogation of the priests, who insisted she must have heard the term previously, Bernadette truthfully

2. Eph 2:18.
3. Werfel, *Song*, 79.
4. Werfel, *Song*, 297–98.

professed her ignorance. The doctrine had only been defined four years before, and this poor peasant girl had never heard of it.

Sometime later, Bernadette was questioned by a disbelieving bishop, who asked for an exact account of her experiences with the lady. She chose to act out her answer, imitating the lady and herself in her rapturous encounter. I like to pause and imagine the scene: this teenaged peasant girl, scrutinized by an informed, critical cleric. The bishop wept.[5] He wept at the mere *imitation* of what the lady had done, at the sheer beauty of it.

What would it mean if this was truly a catholic feast, a catholic vision— catholic in the sense that it reached out to everyone, included everyone?

I believe it does. I believe that when we emerged from the waters of baptism, we were all born again from the womb of our mother church without sin. Born to live a new life, so different from the divisions and dominations that characterize the old life of the kingdoms of this world. I believe that in the sacrament of baptism we were all immaculately conceived. The peasant woman Mary is calling on us to look with the eyes of faith into the gift of the life of Christ held within each of us, as she herself held the life of Jesus in her womb.

Such a grace is not earned, as Mary did not earn her immaculate conception. It is a free gift given to all of us believers. This gift of a new life, an all-embracing life, came from the God who so loved the world through his love of this woman. God wishes all of us other disciples to *live* this new life that God first of all entrusted to Mary. She really is the first to bring that new life to the other believers.

God chose Mary to welcome the beginning of his life-giving, liberating embrace for all the disciples. And, if we were to truly see and listen to the women around us in the church, we might find that the most appropriate response to the story of their lives would be to weep, as did the priest in the story of Bernadette.

I remember how Genesis reads, "And the man called his wife Eve, because she was the mother of all the living."[6] But now when I read that, I hear something new. I hear: "[T]he angel Gabriel was sent by God to a town in Galilee called Nazareth, to a virgin [. . .] the virgin's name was Mary . . ."[7] because *she* is "the mother of all the *living*."

---

5. Werfel, *Song*, 383.
6. Gen 3:20.
7. Luke 1:26–27.

Philip's Reflection

While the words "Immaculate Conception" indicate an important theological doctrine, they also bring a fun memory of my brother and me during one of our many outings. About twenty-five years ago, while I was visiting Simon in Manhattan, we went to see the off-Broadway comedy *Late Nite Catechism*. The audience became part of the production, playing the role of a seventh-grade catechism class taught by an actress who portrays a nun. She asked us questions about Catholic doctrines and rules, and scolded those with incorrect answers or improper grammar. Our "sister" rewarded correct answers by tossing the person a plastic rosary. When she asked us to define the Immaculate Conception, one unlucky soul was chastised when he said it meant that Mary conceived Jesus without human insemination. I raised my hand, and answered that it really meant that Mary was conceived without original sin. After I caught the beads, Simon and I laughed.

Simon's reflection reminded me of his keen awareness and articulation of the many manifestations of oppression, most often enforced with real or threatened violence. He alluded to the harmful effects on women of these oppressive attitudes, with what social justice theorists call "internalized oppression." This occurs when the recipient of the institutional and interpersonal oppression subconsciously accepts, then lives according to the limiting and dehumanizing assignations of the powerful. The person believes and acts in the ways they are cast and personally predict for themselves, producing what psychologists call "self-fulfilling prophecy." Finally, the cycle of oppression is completed and validated by the oppressors when they observe the victimized person subsequently act in the limiting ways first attributed.

God's relationship with Mary is a model of how God's love frees women—and everyone—of all societal and self-imposed constraints and false separations. Simon proposed that the doctrine of Mary's Immaculate Conception is an invitation into the promise of unity in the kingdom of God.

Although Mary was certainly specially blessed, she was not superhuman. If we place her, or anyone, on a pedestal, we dehumanize the person, and that person's imagined "perfection" creates an unattainable state. Since we can never be perfect like the idealized, we absolve ourselves from growth. That inertia is captured in the Voltaire-attributed quote, "Perfect is the enemy of good."[8] Mary, an ordinary person, possessed extraordinary

8. Voltaire Quotes.

courage, strength, and faith, and those are qualities we can prayerfully ask God to deepen in us. Come to think of it, all the early disciples were ordinary people. We too do not need to be famous, to have so many "likes" on social media platforms, for God to love and grace us. We do not have to become anything else to earn God's love. Jesus is always present to embrace us, and work with us, just as we are in each moment.

Bernadette is also a model for us. After reporting her visions, she received unimaginably cruel torments from family, townspeople, teachers, and clergy. Yet she continued to rely on the truth and reality of her own relationship with the lady. I am inspired by her simple, steadfast courage and commitment. She would not be vanquished by much more learned people. Before she finally entered the convent, a psychiatrist briefly interviewed Bernadette. Unaware of his own confirmation bias, he hastily determined she should be institutionalized so that she could be healed of her "mental illness," and inanely told her that subsequently she would be better equipped to deal with life. Nonviolently, and in steely faith, she stared at him and said, "I'm not one bit afraid of that struggle [of life]."[9] Though she was specially chosen, we too can pray for the receptivity to a life-changing relationship with Mary. Perhaps if we listen carefully, we too will hear Mary move us towards "penitence," and urge us to "pray for sinners . . .[and] for the sick world."[10] Mary always leads us to her son, reminding us to "Do whatever he tells you."[11]

Simon proposed an unusual (to me, anyway) understanding that like Mary, we can accept God's invitation to "grow" and nurture Jesus within us. As Mary birthed him, she brought to the world traits of the new life of God's kingdom, such as divinely boundless love, justice and liberation for the oppressed, compassion, mercy, and inclusion. If we also help bring these traits into the world, we participate in a baptism, or immersion, of those healing powers so that we become kingdom-builders in what we say and do. Our new, "immaculately conceived" life unites us with Mary and all those in God's eternal kingdom.

What is of God is life-affirming, enriching, fulfilling, and unifying—both intra- and interpersonally. Jesus' earthly mother provides us with a model by which we may elect to answer God's personal invitation, so that we too can manifest, channel, glorify, and fully participate in the

9. Werfel, *Song*, 378.

10. Werfel, *Song*, 200.

11. John 2:5; Mary's last quoted words in the Gospels.

communion of all God's people. I am filled with gratitude to Mary for her faithfulness, and desire to engage with the Holy Spirit in also carrying Jesus within me, and bringing him into the world.

The nonviolent kingdom of God asks us to freely choose an immeasurably beneficial option: to be a channel for God's unconditional, fully liberating graces.

Questions to Consider: What is the Immaculate Conception? How might Mary's Immaculate Conception foreshadow God's kingdom? How is our own baptism a grace and an empowerment? What is internalized oppression? What happens to a person, and to us, when we place anyone "on a pedestal"? What makes Mary blessed? How is Mary similar to and different from us? Should we strive to become like Mary? Why or why not? If so, how, specifically?

2

Why Was Joseph Afraid? (Matthew 1:18–25)

We begin by recognizing the oppressive and limiting gender roles that Mary's culture maintained, especially for women pregnant outside of marriage. Christian disciples are challenged and understandably fearful when choosing to break away from familiar but oppressive social structures, such as patriarchy. We explore the causes of Joseph's fears within the context of his intergenerationally patriarchal society. God's incarnation explodes social structures that foster limiting, oppressive, and unjust gender roles. Even more, God invites us to see women as uniquely capable of bearing God's presence. Disciples are wise to notice that fear is a great obstacle to loving ourselves and others as Jesus did. Joseph and Mary are primary models of seeking greater faith in God to overcome socially constructed constraints, and all fears.

Breaking the Patriarchy

IN ALL THIS READING for Matthew's Christmas vigil, I want to focus on the words of the angel to Mary's betrothed: "Joseph . . . do not be afraid . . ."[1] We often think of Joseph as the "strong, silent type." And we know that he was a just and prayerful man. Even more, we know that men learn to be men from their earliest days by imitating their fathers. God must have thought great things of Joseph if God chose Joseph to be the model for his Son.

1. Matt 1:20.

7

Yet here we learn that Joseph was afraid. He must have been afraid. Why else would the angel have said to him, "Do not be afraid," unless he was afraid. Joseph *was* afraid. How is it that such a holy and just man could be afraid?

I believe that the hint of an answer is in the reading before the story: all that patriarchy, approved by God, a parade of fathers and sons marching through time, moving toward the birth of the Messiah, finally to arrive at Matthan, the father of Jacob, the father of Joseph, the husband of Mary. But when the Messiah *did* come, he came outside the patriarchy previously ordained by God. Joseph was suddenly "out of the loop" when it came to bringing the savior to the world. It was between this woman Mary and God, and them alone.

That was *such* a change from the socially and religiously, and even divinely, established order of things, that Joseph was frightened. It meant that women, independently of men's will or say-so, independently of men's authority or men's protection (and usually that meant protection from other men), independently of men's social or even biological input, women were now going to bring forth a new presence of God. And Mary really was going to body forth the fullest presence of God, one that—God was saying—the long-standing practices of patriarchy were incapable of producing.

Thus, the Gospel is announcing that from the very conception of Jesus, men and women are going to have to look at each other differently. And especially that men would have to see women as capable of a unique bearing of the presence of God.

That can be frightening to men—even the most just and prayerful men. In one extreme case, for example, American men had poured boiling water down the throats of the early suffragist women looking for the vote. These did not act as just or prayerful men. They were men afraid that the women were escaping their imagined control and so sought to strike out against them in their fear, to force them into the old oppressive structures. And that fear is not a fear confined to American men of the early twentieth century. I believe that we could find such a fear right now in the world. Right now, even in our Catholic Church. I believe that women, even women in the Catholic Church, might fear this freedom.

Joseph, however, answered his fear not with violence but with trust—acting in faith upon what the angel had told him. And it was in that decision of faith that his true paternity lay.

It's the same for all of us. Especially in the life of the Spirit, the life of the faithful, it is not biological parenthood, but the decision we make in faith—sometimes make every day—that we turn away from the old structures of this world, that we turn away from the violence required to defend them, that we turn and instead become members of the family of God. Can we decide in faith, to allow our understanding of ourselves to be completely, completely changed? Can we decide to allow our understanding of what it means to be a man, what it means to be a woman, to be completely, completely changed? Are we ready to have our relationships—even our whole societal structure—completely transformed by a new non-patriarchal, non-violent, motherly presence of God?

In short, are we willing, as Joseph was, to take Mary and Jesus into our hearts, our homes, our lives? Don't be afraid.

Philip's Reflection

Simon was a tireless advocate for freedom, because he believed that that is what Jesus deeply wants for us. He consistently routed out both the obvious and more disguised forms of oppression and enslavement. Here, Simon identified people's tendency to rely on a social patriarchy that is woefully insufficient to host God, literally and figuratively. Patriarchy cannot exist within God's kingdom.

Patriarchy and other exclusionary social constructs are often cultural and traditional. People who benefit from those power inequities justify such constructs as "common sense." Our reflections here, and throughout, encourage readers to challenge commonly held beliefs in the light of Jesus' words and actions.

Tradition does not necessarily produce truth, nor does a majority's opinion. In fact, traditions can be inherently dehumanizing and disempowering. Shirley Jackson's short story "The Lottery" illustrates the fatal effects of relying on intergenerational tradition, to the dramatic exclusion of critical thought, compassion, and morality.[2]

How do our fears of personal safety, affiliation, and survival interfere with trusting God and acting as Joseph did? Surely God understands that fear is a major obstacle in loving as God wants for us, and in building God's kingdom. I found phrases like "Fear not" mentioned in the New Testament

2. Jackson, "Lottery."

at least sixty-two times.[3] Fear may be our single, most formidable obstacle to loving in an "agapeistic" way. Simon's focus on Joseph's fear in the face of the harmful cultural and physical consequences to his pregnant betrothed, encourages us to remember that when we invite God into our struggle, God will comfort and guide us. Faith is a powerful antidote to fear.

Although I wonder what Joseph might have said that was not recorded in the Scriptures, what he *did* reminds me of the power of grace-filled actions in building God's kingdom. He provided a home that nurtured the divine. Subsequently, the one he raised grew to dismantle those social structures which scared Joseph and oppressed so many others.

Tom McMurray, SJ, reminds me that the Scriptures are largely about remembering how God has worked, and that the Gospels are invitations to tell others the wonderful things God has done for us. In my faith journey, I am often brought back to John the Baptist's and Jesus' admonitions to repent, and to seek to change my mind to the mind of God, through Christ.[4]

How often must Jesus have felt doubt, loss, and fear, and confronted it with prayer and great faith in his heavenly Father? I suspect Joseph modeled prayerful abandonment to God's will. What can we do to become more like the Holy Family in times of fear and diminished faithfulness and belief?

Questions to Consider: How do you define a patriarchal society? What connotations does it hold? In what ways is a patriarchal social system similar to the Catholic Church's structure? How do you suppose a patriarchal society compares and contrasts with the kingdom Jesus proclaimed? Do you believe that we earn God's love and grace? What if anything can we do to lose that love and grace? Are there any people or groups of people that are more special to God? Explain. Early in Joseph's relationship with Mary, what scared him? How did Joseph respond to his deep fears? How does Joseph's faith reveal a "true patriarchy"?

The kingdom of God asks that we have the courage and faith to prepare to have our relationships—along with our restrictive and exclusionary societal structures—completely transformed by a new non-patriarchal, nonviolent, motherly presence of God.

---

3. Cruden, *Cruden's Concordance*.

4. See Matt 3:2. The Greek word for repent is *metanoia*, which translated means "change of mind towards a new direction."

3

Jesus Saves Peter and Us on Turbulent Waters (Matthew 14:22–33)

Jesus is pleased to work with us in liberating us from fear and doubt. Jesus asked Peter, who had typical human flaws and weaknesses, to lead his church. When we deepen our friendship and trust in Jesus, we realize that he embraces our humanity, and that no human weakness excludes us from God's love and grace. Jesus is delighted to accept our imperfect efforts to work on his behalf.

Peter on the Water

MARTIN LUTHER KING JR. ended a sermon with the sentence, "Fear knocked on the door. Faith answered. There was no one there."[1] But as I meditated on this passage in Matthew after walking, and then sinking with Peter and I heard Jesus say, "Why did you doubt?,"[2] I felt that he was talking to me about me and my self-doubt. It is an insight I have used often in spiritual direction, harkening back to Isaiah: "I, I am he who comforts you; who are you to be afraid . . . ?"[3]

There was one time I was so frightened, I actually shouted in fear. I wondered afterwards, what instinct caused me to do that? Maybe once,

1. King, *Strength to Love*, 126.
2. Matt: 14:31.
3. Isa 51:12.

back in our evolutionary line, our ancestors tried to shout away beasts and monsters that threatened them—I don't know. But I wonder if that has ever happened to anyone else. Shouting in fear?

I'm wondering because in today's reading in Matthew the apostles were shouting in fear. But that's the middle of the story. I want to pick it up from the beginning.

Jesus has just miraculously fed thousands of men, women, and children who had no food. Miraculously, because the only ones who secured any food were the apostles—and they had only five loaves and two fish. But Jesus blessed the food, broke the bread, and gave it to all the disciples. And everyone ate and had enough.

Then Jesus made his apostles get into the boat, and he himself went up to a mountain to pray. The boat was being tossed around on a rough sea, and then, somewhere between three and six AM, the apostles saw Jesus walking toward them on the sea. I try to visualize that: walking on the water.

They were terrified—"It is a ghost!"—and the whole group of them began shouting out in fear.[4] Imagine it: grown men, fishermen who had probably seen their share of terrors on the sea, shouting with fear. Well, scaring us is never Jesus' intention; he was just trying to catch up with these guys. So he immediately reassures them: "Get a grip on yourselves. It's me. Don't be afraid." One of them, Peter, decided to follow the Lord's command not to be afraid. But he had a particular way of overcoming his fear. Peter charged right at the thing that was making him afraid.

I have to confess: that's the way I handle things that frighten me. "Lord, if it is you," Peter said, "command me to come to you on the water."[5] Pause for a dramatic moment here: what's going to happen next?

Jesus simply says, "Okay, Peter, come on!" What's Peter going to do now? He's got no other option than to follow where his mouth has led him. He's out of the boat and walking toward Jesus. But then he saw the wind and the waves and got scared and . . .

Another dramatic pause as I imagine what was going through Peter's mind. Imagining that I'm Peter. What might be going through his mind, walking on the water with all that wind and those high waves? It seems to me that Peter would be saying to himself, "Me and my big mouth! I always do this. I always talk before I think. I talk myself into trouble and here I am again. This wind is going to knock me down, and the waves are going

4. See Matt 14:26.
5. Matt 14:28.

to drown me and I can't swim and what in the heck was I thinking when I said that?" And Peter started sinking. "Lord!" he cried out, "Save me!"[6] Did Jesus wait a while longer, to teach him a lesson? No, thank God, Jesus is not a teacher like that. Nope: immediately—immediately—Jesus grabs Peter by the hand and raises him up. Not until Peter was standing again did Jesus teach him the lesson: "You of little faith, why did you doubt?"[7]

What exactly was Peter supposed to learn? What are people like me supposed to learn from Jesus' words to Peter? First part of the lesson: don't get so involved with yourself that you forget to look for Jesus. And the second part: I think that Jesus was saying to Peter, "Peter, I know you. I know that you talk before you think. I knew you were going to ask that. I knew you would, so I made the water firm for you so that you could walk on it. I had you covered—why did you doubt?"

Why did you doubt that I could work with someone like you?

And isn't that the question? Isn't that the lesson for all of us disciples? Don't we get so self-involved that we fail to attend to the call of Jesus? Don't we look at our faults and failings and then doubt that God can work through us? No need to look far: when we hear the commands of Jesus, to "love your enemies,"[8] for example, aren't we tempted to say, "Not me; I could never do that, I've got a real bad temper; that's for idealists and saints and holy people." When we hear the great promises of Jesus, "Your Father is pleased to give you the kingdom,"[9] aren't we tempted to say, "Yeah, for someone else, for priests and nuns maybe. Not me"? Why do we doubt that God can work with someone like us?

Maybe we can ask Jesus—and Peter—to teach us this lesson: "Christ Jesus came into the world to save sinners."[10] Keep looking to him. He's got us covered. He knows us, he knows our sins, he knows we're going to mess up, and he's still got our backs. He's never going to abandon us. He "will command his angels concerning you to guard you in all your ways."[11] All our ways.

Why do we doubt?

6. Matt 14:30.
7. Matt 14:31.
8. Matt 5:44.
9. Luke 12:32.
10. 1 Tim 1:15.
11. Ps 91:11 (CCB).

Philip's Reflection

Simon reminded me that Jesus calls on powers that calm external and internal storms. According to the brilliant apologist for Christian nonviolence, Fr. Emmanuel Charles McCarthy, power can be defined philosophically as having the ability to bring about change.[12] Most of us equate power with dominative force, as my high school students always did. While dominative power through violence or threat of violence indeed can bring about change, there are many other powers that do not threaten, diminish, or destroy life. Kindness and compassion are also powers. What powers course through God's kingdom?

The greatest power is the constant, unconditional, and welcoming love of the Trinity as incarnated in Jesus. Emanating with that love are powers such as compassion, healing, forgiveness, kindness, generosity, and other life-enriching realities. Our God does not let us drown. Nor does God use violence or threat of harm.

At times, I let my doubts and fears occupy center stage. I get fooled by the apparent victories and ubiquitous use of dominative violence, and despair in the failures of nonviolence to replace all institutional and state violence. When I do not invite Jesus to be with me at those times and look for his friendship and presence, perhaps like Peter on the waters, I start to metaphorically sink in the stormy seas of *only* what I can see, think, or feel. Within that struggle, the evil spirit gleefully attaches the litany of self-recriminating statements, past failures, future dread, diminishment, and further doubt. His added weights sink me further. Worse yet, I doubt that such a weakened person can be of value or use to Jesus.

Jesus overrides those desolations and temptations. The shortcomings, the illusory sense of separation from God that is part of sinfulness, our personal history of failings, losses, unanswered questions, regrets, and the other waves of the turbulent seas, hasten our sinking. But Jesus knows each of us, as he did Peter. The lie is that we need to be perfect, or always without doubt or temptation, to be acceptable and valuable to him. And what's more, our woundedness does not need to disappear for us to be compassionate with ourselves, and to be loved by God.

Tom McMurray, SJ, reminded me that the resurrected Jesus still bore the wounds from the cross and the torture by the soldiers. Our wounded

---

12. See McCarthy, "Behold the Lamb," a thorough, transformational retreat on Jesus and his nonviolent message. I urge readers to examine his website, as it contains a plethora of his written and visual materials, all gratis.

places don't disappear. Rather, they are transformed through divine grace. When we reach to Jesus, he will lift us from our woundedness, doubt, and infiltration by the evil spirit. It may help each of us to identify our own self-limiting thoughts and doubts, like the ones Simon mentioned in his life. Am I smart enough to protest nuclear weapons or climate change? Am I faithful enough to challenge a racist remark? Can I face the attacks from those who support divisiveness and hatred and other activities counter to the kingdom of God? Jesus will work with us as we are; our cooperation with his will—not our success—is our gift to God.

We just need to call his name and reach out to grasp his extended hand.

Questions to Consider: In this passage from Matthew, with whom do you most identify, and why? What methods did Jesus use to reveal himself, and to further teach his disciples? Why do you imagine that Peter sought to walk on the water? Why did he sink? When you are buffeted by life's storms, what do you tend to do, and not do? How and when does your faith in God typically come into consciousness? What makes us metaphorically "sink" during our walk with Jesus?

God's perpetual, unconditional love, which is omnipresent and ever-nourishing, is the greatest power in the nonviolent kingdom of God.

4

Jesus Faithfully Searches for All to Return to the Kingdom (Luke 15:1–11)

We emphasize that God's call to enter the kingdom includes everyone, where each is truly welcomed and equal. We can work towards building that kingdom on earth, as it is in heaven, by rejecting social assignments of inferiority to targeted social identities such as race, gender, and ethnicity. Since God desires us to know our authentic selves and to be free, God's kingdom is in direct contrast with every limiting and diminishing role imposed by others. We should strive to be cognizant of our own separation and sinfulness, and call out for Jesus who searches for the lost. Like Jesus, we too can search for and invite all people into God's community, especially the marginalized and forgotten. We should also invite those who have oppressed them and cast them out.

The Lost Sheep and the Lost Coin

WHEN YOU LEARN TO pray as a Jesuit, you begin by imagining the scenes of the gospel. Something like when we make the Stations of the Cross, except that instead of an artist conceiving of the scenes, you imagine them. Even though Ignatius pretty much leaves it to the imagination of the one praying, it always helps me to situate the gospel in the real, historic setting of Jesus' own life, as far as I can know it.

Let's listen to Jesus as he speaks to us, once again, of the reign of our compassionate God. First, let's look at the crowd. There are men, women, and children there, pretty much all of them poor, and all of them listening to the words of the one they perceived was going to liberate them from occupation by the Roman Empire. We notice two things right away. The first thing we can envision is that, according to the customs of that time, the men and women sat in separate groups. Are they separate and unequal? Not according to Jesus! Look how he addresses each group equally. First, he turns to the men and says, "Which of you, having lost a single sheep from the flock . . ." And then he turns to the women and says, "Which of you, having lost a single coin in her house . . . ?" Speaking to them each equally with scenes from their own experience of the insistent, we might even say relentless, forgiveness of God.[1]

First to the men. I think it might take me a bit longer to understand what Jesus is saying to the men. But that's okay because—and both Judaism and Islam tell us this—men need more instruction in the spiritual life than women who, because they are life-bearers, know instinctively and immediately what God is talking about. So he talks to the men about shepherds—again, a lower class of people in that culture.

Once when I was in Jamaica, as I was wandering around the hills, I saw a shepherd and of course I started to speak to him. He told me that sheep are really "herd" animals. They don't have a really deep brain pan (he didn't say that; I'm summarizing), and they rely on the other herd members and the shepherd for guidance and security. He told me they are so skittish that they are always milling about, sniffing, peering around—nervous, afraid that something's going to come after them. They almost never lie down, except in two instances. The first is if the shepherd has led them to a place where they sense no danger, absolutely no danger anywhere. No matter how much they sniff or listen or look, they find no danger at all. After a while of feeling perfectly safe, the sheep may lie down. That's where we get the image in the Twenty-Third Psalm, "[The Lord is my shepherd] . . . in verdant pastures he gives me repose."[2] The other time that sheep will lie down is more dangerous. If the sheep gets separated from the flock and shepherd, its physical disconnection becomes a kind of psychological disorientation. Confused, frustrated, lost, and profoundly helpless, it will just plop down on the ground. Plop!

Bad enough. But then, if it lies down in a dip in the field, even a small indentation, it can roll over onto its side and get stuck there. It's kicking its

1. Luke 15:4,8.
2. Ps 23:1–2.

little stick-legs, but it can't get back up. That's called being "cast" or "cast down." We hear that image referred to in the Forty-Second Psalm: "Why are you so downcast, O my soul?"[3] Then the problem is that the insides of the sheep start to shift over, and it can suffocate on its own insides. Can the reader relate to that image, to what it feels like when it's what's inside that is killing you?

I think it's no coincidence that our word "sin" comes from the German word "Sünde," which means "separation." We have another cognate of the German in English: "sunder." As in, "What God has joined together, let no man put asunder." That's the nature of sin. It's not something fun that followers of Jesus don't get a chance to do. It's a reality that rends us, tears us from God, tears us from others, and tears us even from ourselves. Sin is a reality that isolates and disorients us, and eventually it will kill us.

Well, then the shepherd only has a little time to rescue the sheep before it dies. That's the background of this story, so understandable to these poor folk, and a powerful way for Jesus to present the urgency he feels to find and carry back those who have become separated from his Father.

Now Jesus turns to the group of women. Look at your homes. He said to them, You know how your dirt floors are packed down with the dregs of the olive oil pressings. Keeps the dust down, yes, but it makes the floors so dark, doesn't it? And with just small holes in the walls for windows, what happens? You can't see a coin if you drop it. We poor folks can't afford to lose even a single coin. I mean, wouldn't it be bizarre to say, "Oh well, I've got nine others—who cares?" Who would say that? So you take out the broom and sweep, sweep, sweep—everywhere—until you find it. I imagine the impoverished Mary saying to her son, "I've got to sweep until I find this lost coin. If you want to stay, help me look for it. On your hands and knees, son! Help me find that lost coin."

Let's imagine once more that we are in the crowd after we have heard Jesus speak and as we walk back to our flocks and our homes, we begin reflecting on what he said to us. Let me tell you what I was thinking as I walked away from this sermon of his. First is that the crowd was waiting for Jesus to show them the kingdom and the power and the glory—power enough to lead us out of domination by the Empire. But Jesus surprises us by taking ordinary things from everyday life and saying, Open your eyes and see: the kingdom is right here, arising out of the life of the poor and oppressed. There's no need to go outside our own experience to find the

3. Ps 42:6, 12.

18

dynamics of liberation or to look for any other leadership than that of the Spirit among us.

What is the nature of the power of that liberating Spirit? It's the spirit of forgiveness, of bringing back into community. Not a cute "no problem" kind of forgiveness. Not a "forget it" kind of reconciliation. The Spirit surely recognizes that there's major trouble, even lethal difficulties here: if we don't find the one who is lost, the one who is separated, then he or she could become cast down to death.

We understand the reason that Jesus doesn't respond to the sinner with punishment and dismissal, much less violence or retribution! Look at the sheep: the sinner is already being punished by the sin, by the separation itself. Whether it's our own sin, or the sin of a friend, or the sin of an enemy who is oppressing us, Jesus wants us to understand that that sin is killing them. That is surely an act of faith, because the world teaches us that the ability to cause pain, the capacity to inflict death means that someone is powerful. No, says Jesus! Their domination over the poor, their separation from the Spirit of community, means they are separating themselves from the Shepherd and it's killing them. What should you do now if you love them? You can't let them suffocate to death! You love them. You love your enemies too much to let them die by harming you or others. Like a shepherd—like the Good Shepherd—we must stride out like men who have the courage and vision to seek out, rescue, and reconcile our separated brother, bearing him back into the community.

And like women, we must search diligently because we know that to recover our sister is to enrich ourselves. What's more, we must search with prayer. Because look at Mary, teaching Jesus how to seek out and find what was lost. From his life in Mary's household, Jesus offers us an image to comfort and strengthen us in our mission: Jesus will approach the sinner not riding on a steed, not striding down the street, but rising from his knees, having prayed for us.

Today, let us follow the forgiving Jesus as he followed what he learned from his mother: "If you want to stay in this house . . . then get on your knees, Child of the Most High God. On your knees and help me look for what is lost."[4]

4. Cf. Luke 19:10.

19

Philip's Reflection

The Word of God certainly proclaims immediate and eternal relevance, and Simon contextualized the gospel, making it easier to apply to today's realities. In this passage, Jesus begins by acknowledging his people's desperation, then liberates us from it by telling us about God's kingdom. We can appreciate the various forms of oppression that imprison us. Poverty violates human dignity; it isolates and separates. Institutional impoverishment—a tool of the occupiers and power elites, or "owning class"—is a form of violence that erodes body and spirit. Jesus wants our liberation from that, wants his followers to identify with and meet the needs of the poor, and desires our freedom from any internal and external constraint.

The lost sheep, inextricably linked to the herd and its shepherd, is suffering from isolation. When we sin, or think and act in ways in opposition to the herd—God's kingdom—even though we may find others with us, we are on the outside, leading to death. The Shepherd, Jesus, sets out in haste to save each of us from dying. In God's kingdom, those saved imitate the Shepherd by searching for anyone—even enemies—to redress *their* pain of separation and potential death. Prayerfully reflecting on God's unfathomable mercy, faithfulness, and love for me, and for all of us, moves me to seek even small ways to do the same for all others. I start by acting nonviolently with my family and friends, in accordance with Pope Francis's assertion that "it is fundamental that nonviolence be practiced before all else within families."[5]

As a social justice educator, I apply these parables to today's gender roles. Males and females have distinctly differing frames of reference, and use words to capture their experiences in different ways. Jesus is on a loving mission to save all, regardless of how we express ourselves. Jesus will use what the Father created to access our authentic selves. Perhaps we are most accessible to God when we are searching for something that is important to us. That desire for completion is a focus of Simon's first book.[6] In it, he references Aquinas, Ignatius, and others to substantiate the postulation that God created us with deep passions, which naturally move us toward something. Rather than shunning them, we can align our passions to move us towards completion within God.

5. Francis, "Nonviolence," 4.
6. Harak, *Virtuous Passions.*

Jesus again demonstrates his essential reliance on his Father. These parables reiterate how important we are to the Trinity. God seeks to bring us back to the fold and to restore our losses. The next time I feel isolated, lost, or separated, I hope to pray to return quickly to these two examples of the kingdom, listening for his urgent call for me. To paraphrase the Bard, when "I think on [the Good Shepherd], all [my] losses are restored and sorrows end."[7]

Questions to Consider: Identify details you know or can imagine concerning the image of Jesus as the Good Shepherd. How can we act like the Good Shepherd today? What are the ways in which we can pass along to friends and enemies God's love and mercy for each of us? Does Jesus want for his followers to seek to reconcile with *all* our enemies? If so, why? If not, why not? What literary or other artistic works parallel the Good Shepherd or the parable of the lost coin, and the pearl of great price? During Jesus' time on earth, what were the cultural and societal ways in which women were treated differently than men? How can poverty imprison people? How does God's Spirit deliver or liberate us from sin?

The kingdom of God is designed by a loving God who will search tirelessly and urgently for anyone who is outside of it.

7. Shakespeare, Sonnet 30, lines 13–14.

5

Sharing the Christ-Life within Us
(Luke 2:1–20)

*Let us consider the proposition that Christmas is not merely the day
we remember Jesus' birth. We also celebrate that on that day, Christ is
born in each one of us. Consequently, each of us is entrusted by God
to give the Christ-life, the Spirit within us, words to speak. God wants
us to find our own words for our inner life, since that Christ-life lives
uniquely within each of us. Here, we share several ways that we can
discover the vocabulary for God within us.*

A Midnight Mass Reflection

I WOULD LIKE TO invite all of us to visit Mary and Joseph and the infant
Jesus who lies in the manger. And let us begin by approaching the child
with the same tenderness and wonder that we would approach any child.
What do the parents and relatives and friends of a newborn infant first look
for?

Well, you put your finger into the baby's palm, yes, and see if the baby
grips your finger. And when he does, you always comment to the parents
on how *strong* the baby is. And then the parents look for the first smile,
don't they? Sometimes mothers keep a journal of first things for their baby,
and they'll record, "Today my daughter smiled for the first time." Of course
they do that only for the first baby. After that they notice, I'm sure, but really, it's too much trouble . . .

But this was Mary and Joseph's firstborn son, and they were looking attentively for these things—as all parents do, as we might do: the grip on the finger, the first smile . . . and the first *word* that the infant says. Maybe it's "Da-Da" or "Ma-Ma." Or maybe "garbage truck." Sometimes mothers and fathers must be good linguists, good interpreters, to understand what their baby is saying. But let's look, let's listen with Mary and Joseph for Jesus' first word. Let's listen to them try to teach the infant Jesus to speak. Watch them patiently repeat words over and over so that the infant Jesus can learn to talk.

And this is an ironic and wonderful thing when we think of it, isn't it? We believe that Jesus is the Word of God, don't we? Yes, he is the Word become flesh. And yet here we are at the manger with Mary and Joseph and the infant Jesus, and Jesus cannot speak. The Word of God has no words. In fact, that's what the word "infant" means in Latin. It means "not talking." "In-fans"—"no speech." Here is the Word of God, and he cannot speak.

Here is the Word of God, and God is relying on Mary and Joseph to give his Son the right words, the right way to express himself, to bring forth his heart, to present his inner self, his spirit to the world. Because without them, with these human beings, the Word of God would have no speech at all. We can imagine Mary and Joseph through the years: "How did you feel about that? Are you angry, are you sad? You look very happy today. Did you enjoy playing with your friends today?" Human beings, teaching the Word of God to speak.

And didn't they teach him well! Remember when Mary was outlining God's social program and she said, "He has thrown down the rulers from their thrones but lifted up the lowly"?[1] So thirty years later, her son had learned to say, "Blessed are you who are poor," and "But woe to you who are rich."[2] Do you remember when Mary praised God and said, "The Mighty One has done great things for me, and holy is his name"?[3] Well, thirty years later, when his disciples asked Jesus to teach them to pray, he said, "Say, 'Our Father in heaven, hallowed be your name.'"[4] Where did he learn such words? From Mary, from his human mother.

And what about Joseph? In all the Scripture, we don't hear Joseph utter a single word. Perhaps because he was more of a man of action. Perhaps

1. Luke 1:52.
2. Luke 6:20, 24.
3. Luke 1:49.
4. Matt 6:9.

Joseph was more of a doer. Joseph the worker—the man of deeds. And maybe from Joseph, Jesus learned to express himself in another way—by actions, by deeds. His healing, his repair of his Father's broken creation, his working of miracles to feed his new spiritual family, his courage to stand against the oppression of the Roman Empire—even his overcoming the crude carpentry of the cross. I believe these powerful works expressing his soul came from Joseph, his human father.

And why is this important to us? Because when we were baptized, when we were confirmed, God put the seed of God's own life within us. And God is trusting us—us human beings—to give words to that new life within us. On Christmas we celebrate that Christ is born in each one of us, and it is we who are entrusted by God to give the Christ-life, the Spirit within us, words to speak.

Where might we find such sacred words? We start off by prayer. You know that we start praying by imitating and memorizing the words we hear our parents and godparents and faith community members say. We hardly know what they mean at first. Sometimes it takes a whole lifetime to understand them. But it's like the infant, imitating the words of her parents, learning to speak in that way. The God-life within us learns first to speak by prayers, and later to speak more truthfully by understanding those prayers we pray.

And of course, in the Scripture. Scripture is written by people who listened deeply to the word of God within and expressed it. In their words, we can find deep resonances of the words that the Christ-life within us so longs to speak. We sometimes hear the right words in spiritual conversations with friends. Someone will speak and we say out loud or to ourselves, "Oh, that is what *I* feel; that is what *I* believe," and so we find better and better vocabulary for the Spirit within. And how important it is for us to find our *own* words for our inner life. For the Christ-life lives uniquely, uniquely in each one of us. By listening deeply to our own heart, we can discover the speech, the vocabulary, and the words of God within us.

Let me remind you of something else when you're teaching a child to speak. You know that if you use one wrong word once—one dirty word or swear word or curse word—the child picks it right up and begins to use it over and over. And especially around company. Embarrassing! You know, there are bad words for the Christ-life with us, too. "War" is one. It doesn't fit that Christ-life within us. Here's another: "death penalty." Whoa! Those are *two* words together that are bad words for a Christian trying to express the Christ-life within. "Death" and "penalty" both! Just as you often take months to have a child "unlearn" bad words, so it may take a long time for the God-life within to "unlearn" words like that, to purify our spirits so that we can present the peaceful, loving, forgiving, resurrecting Christ within us once again to the world.

On Christmas we celebrate the infant Jesus. That day, and every day, we can begin to imagine ourselves listening to Mary and Joseph—these simple human beings—holding hands, smiling, teaching the Word of God to speak. And I would like it if we, poor human beings that we are, could go forth with our own mission, similar to theirs: Give your own words to the Word of God born within. Teach the Christ-life within you to speak.

Philip's Reflection

Simon skillfully uses his words to express the beauty of the newborn Word of God within each of us. I resonate with three aspects of his meditation.

Each day, and with each interpersonal and social interaction, we have a chance to say the words of Christ, and to be a person of faith-based action. We can choose to act as Mary and Joseph did by nurturing the infant Jesus, speaking back to him his words. How? By praying standard prayers, by conversing with God in our words, by listening to the words of the Scripture, by loving and caring for God's creation, by maintaining a livable space for God within us, and by acting with kindness and mercy to all we interact with.

But how are we to be certain that the words we express are truly Christ-centered? Ignatius talks of the necessity of discernment in his Spiritual Exercises.[5] Frequent prayer, deep reflection on the Scriptures, and an attentive and active community of believers helps discern the movement of the Spirit. We must also pray for the ongoing courage to be mindful of our own internal dynamics, to look fearlessly at the fruits of our thoughts and actions. Do they lead to harmony, peace, reconciliation, mercy, forgiving love, and compassion? If they do not, or if they lead to distress, anxiety, anger, fear, confusion, and the like, we can be confident that those negative feelings and attendant actions are not coming from what Ignatius called the "good spirits." We must continually open the metaphoric door to Jesus in

5. See O'Brien, *Ignatian Adventure*, 115–18, for a good concise explanation. Ignatius believed that we all have "motions of the soul" that were the result of "good spirits and evil spirits."

all that we do. He always invites himself into my life in its current state, and asks that I share who I am with him.

The second aspect is that the words used so freely by many disciples in our culture have a powerful "anti-Christ" impact. Words like "I hate those people," "I'll never forgive," and the like. Simon invited us to "teach the Christ-life within [us] to speak." I ask Christians who advocate for exclusion, violence, and other forms of domination, fear, and hatred, to pray to the Trinity to verify the presence of Christ in those words and desires. Christians who argue with me about the validity of justified violence have failed to provide New Testament support for that position. There exists no legitimate image of Jesus as warrior.[6] Instead, I urge them to prayerfully contemplate Pope Benedict's words that for Christians "nonviolence is a person's way of being, the attitude of one who is *so convinced of God's love and power* that he or she is not afraid to tackle evil with the weapons of love and truth alone."[7]

The third aspect is of a metacognitive nature. Simon's illness prevented him from publishing his scriptural meditations, and it rendered him silent during his last years. By presenting his words, I maintain a literal conversation with him, with you, and with God. Consequently, as I add my words about God to Simon's, we brothers give praise to the God who raised him, healed him, and listens to his eternal words of praise.

Questions to Consider: Reflect on the reality that God's Son came into this world as a baby. What images, details come to mind when imagining Jesus as an infant, then a toddler? How does caring for a human infant provide us with ways to care for Jesus? How might we disciples give our own words to the Word of God born within each of us? Can you imagine words and/ or actions that the adult Jesus expressed that may have reflected Mary and Joseph?

In God's kingdom, it is important for us to find and to speak our own, authentic words for the Christ-life that resides uniquely within each of us.

---

6. As Fr. Charles McCarthy has pointed out, no Christian argues that Jesus taught a principle of random violence. The debate is whether he taught absolute nonviolence, or violence justified under certain circumstances.

7. Benedict, "Angelus," lines 13–14.

6

Whom Do We Hear When Jesus Calls the Twelve Disciples?

(Matt 4:18–22; Mark 1:16–20, 2:13–17;
Luke 5:1–11, 27–33; John 1:35–51)

As our faith and friendship in Jesus deepens, we move towards apostleship. These next twelve chapters reflect on the deepening of our relationship with Jesus, and specific ways to live it. This chapter explores two aspects of our developing friendship with Jesus. First, Jesus entrusts us to act based upon the power God instilled in us. Second, in direct opposition to warring soldiers, "troops" of God's kingdom are set forth without violence to heal, comfort, and humbly serve others—thereby deepening everyone's humanity.

The Calling of the Twelve Disciples

COMING FROM MIDDLE EASTERN heritage, I have always appreciated the significance of names and naming. My earliest independent reading, I remember, was looking up the meaning of various names. When I meet people, I usually open the conversation by talking about the etymology of their names. In most cases, people are pleased to know what their names mean, and often they nod their heads, acknowledging that their name indeed describes their personality. There is another dimension reflected in this meditation, however. At the end of every meditative scriptural scene,

Ignatius asks us to have a "colloquy," a conversation with some person in the scene. During my first long retreat, I first heard Jesus call my name. It was January 15, 1971.

Once, a long time ago, I was on a retreat in a house far up on the hillside of a beautiful valley. It was an isolated place, and there were only a few houses below in the valley. One day, as I was praying on the porch overlooking the valley, a mother came out of one of the homes and called to her son. It was evening, and perhaps she was calling him home for a meal. "Michael!" she called. But I cannot express the way she said it. There was such a tone of mother's care in her call, such a history of love. And her voice had the slightest twinge of urgency to it. Not fear, not even anxiety, really, but you could tell she was concerned that she couldn't see him right away. Where was her son? He needed to come home for supper. "Michael."

It's been over thirty years and I still remember her call. I remember how, even though it was gentle, her voice somehow carried over the whole valley and reached up even to the side of the hill where I was praying. I think her call was memorable not only because it reached my ears from so far away, but also because it touched my heart.

I believe that is what has happened today, when Jesus calls his twelve apostles. He calls them by name. And yes, they hear his words, but their hearts are touched as well. When he pronounces their names, it moves their souls in a way that no other has ever moved it—not even the call of their father or mother.

I remember how John in his Gospel tells of first meeting Jesus. He told of how when he came up to Jesus, he asked him, "Rabbi, where are you staying?"[1] I think that perhaps John wasn't sure what to say to this man whom John the Baptist had just identified as the savior of the world. And Jesus said to him, "Come and you will see." Fifty years later, John's remark about that first meeting, those first words of Jesus were: "It was about four in the afternoon."[2] I can imagine the impact that that meeting, those simple words, that open invitation had on him. I remember when Jesus first called my name that January. It's not so unusual, I think: After all those years, John still remembered the exact time: *I heard his voice. He spoke to me. Even after all this time, I remember. I remember it was about four in the afternoon . . .*

That was why they followed him. He was calling them to their true home, calling them to the community of God, summoning them to become

1. John 1:38.
2. John 1:39.

what they had somehow known they were meant to be from the day they were born—from the day they were conceived. Named, called, invited, summoned by the one who loved them from before they were born—loved them from all time.

And how about me? Yes, I remember when he first called me. It still "sounds an echo in my soul."[3] And I hope that I follow it still. I somehow always know when it's Jesus: He speaks my name to my soul as no other can.

I think the gospel would like to invite us to turn away from the ones being called to the one doing the calling, because Jesus' experience is always helpful to examine for us who have his Spirit. At the beginning of the passage, Jesus realizes that he simply can't continue to spread the good news by himself. *I can't do this*, he says. *I can't do this anymore; I can't do it alone.* So he asks his disciples to pray to God his Father to send laborers out into the harvest, laborers from the Master of the harvest to help him in the work of the kingdom. But what happens? A little while later, we see that Jesus himself is sending the laborers out into the harvest. And we learn two things from this. The first is clear, that the Master of the harvest is Jesus.

But the second also teaches something. Jesus begins by praying to the Father. But then, after a night of prayer, he finds out that God has named Jesus himself to be the Master of the harvest—that God has conferred this authority to *him*. Doesn't that happen sometimes to us as well? We begin by asking God, sometimes pleading for help: "God help me. I can't do this. I can't go on. You've got to do something for me, God." But then, after we quiet ourselves in prayer, we find out that God has given us the power to solve the problem ourselves. To call our own helpers and assemble our own community. God has taken our weakness and made us strong.

Sometimes, when it seems that God is not doing anything to answer our prayer, it is because he has placed the power to answer our prayer within *us*. In the Gospel of Mark, Jesus teaches, "Therefore I tell you, all that you ask for in prayer, *believe that you will receive it*, and it shall be yours."[4] And in discovering within ourselves that power, that authority, we gain a new understanding of our dignity as daughters and sons of God. That is why, I believe, that after almost all of his healings, Jesus took care to teach, "Your faith [*your* faith] has saved you . . ."[5]

3. Anonymous, "How Can I Keep from Singing?"
4. Mark 11:24, emphasis added.
5. Luke 7:50; 18:42, for example.

Lastly, let's put this call into its historical context. About a half-century before Jesus was born, the undefeatable military legions of the Roman Empire had swept into the small Middle Eastern country of Israel. They had no trouble conquering the country, but a great deal of trouble holding on to it. They had orders to kill the people, to torture them to death—even on a cross. If the people were poor, if they were sick, if they were unemployed, hungry, and robbed of their dignity, then they couldn't resist the empire that came to steal their resources, tax their livelihoods, and degrade their labor, all the while singing that theirs was an ideal and even god-ordained civilization.

When Jesus sends his troops out, it's just the opposite. They are to feed the people that the empire wants hungry, to heal those the empire wants sick, not to kill, not ever to kill, but to raise the people the empire wants dead. And instead of selling their services, the apostles are to give them away for free.[6]

Then, during this life-giving resistance to the powers of death, only then can they proclaim that "the kingdom of God is among you."[7] Not killing, not starving, not "dividing to dominate," not selling this security or citizenship—that's the way of the kingdoms of this world. To feed, to heal, to raise from the dead, to foster and build communities of service—that's the way of the kingdom of God, the way of Jesus.

The way, the truth, and the life.[8]

Now it's tempting for me to think, "Well, that could never be *me*." But the point is that these people, whose names we read today—these people who were fishermen and farmers, outcasts and collaborators—really, they could very well have said the same thing to themselves! But they had then what we have now: like all the disciples, they had the encounter with Jesus. Like us, they had his commands. And like us, they heard him call their names. In fact, I dare to say that we are better off now than were these first-called apostles—better off because we have his Spirit, since the Spirit had not yet been given "because Jesus had not yet been glorified."[9]

6. See Matt 10:8.
7. Luke 17:21.
8. John 14:6.
9. John 7:39.

Philip's Reflection

Simon's story of the mother's call to her son, and later, of Jesus' call to discipleship, reminds me that effective communication requires persistence and mindful, soulful attentiveness. Often, in prayer, I create space for God by stopping and listening to Jesus, or look with opened eyes at his presence beside me. When facing trials, like the mother, I urgently and persistently call to God.[10] James tells us that the trials we face produce perseverance, and if our perseverance is perfect, "you may be perfect and complete, lacking in nothing."[11] God provides us with the power, the resources, and the wisdom to solve our problems. Of course, it is not only my calling, and my power. It is the Holy Spirit within me, who "comes to the aid of our weakness; for we do not know how to pray as we ought, but the Spirit itself intercedes with inexpressible groanings."[12]

We are individually known, loved, and called by Jesus. But much noise interferes with his voice. Some of it is the distraction of daily life. Other loud shouts come from those who encourage us to dismiss and dehumanize "those people," or to hate and harm our enemies. Some interference comes from the internal doubt that says that God is not really involved in our lives, cannot do the impossible, like love us boundlessly as we are, make the broken parts whole, and nonviolently defeat evil and death. I sometimes resist letting Jesus into the darkness. When I turn away from his loving gaze, my woundedness, shame, fear, and despair fuel a sense of isolation. We need to bring our resistance to Jesus, asking at least for the desire to listen. Ignatius reminds us not to contribute to the negative spiraling. Instead, act against the desolation, and prayerfully recall times of God's consoling graces. My relationship and connection with God become deeper when I share my entire self.

I also have experienced moments of the joy and the power of the kingdom of heaven, both alone and with others. Recalling times of painful isolation, but nourished by the grace-filled community, I am propelled to imitate God's love, and share hopefulness, because "if we hope for what we do not see, we wait with endurance."[13]

---

10. See Matt 7:7–8; Mark 11:24; Luke 11:9–10; Jas 1:6–8, for persistence and faith in prayer.

11. Jas 1:3–5.

12. Rom 8:26.

13. Rom 8:25.

Questions to Consider: Are there times when you feel resistant to listening to God? If so, can you notice any factors or patterns around that resistance? What have you done, or observed others do or not do during those resistant times? How might God use our prayer as a way for God to affirm *God's faith in us?* How is Jesus' commission to his disciples similar to and different from those given by the military to their soldiers? Explore the possibility that we are more graced to help build God's kingdom than even his disciples. Can you recall when Jesus called you? How often do you return to that time?

Fortified by God's constant, unconditional love for each of us, Jesus asks us to build and foster communities of service to others.

7

Jesus' Nonviolent Direct Action in the Temple (Luke 19:28–49 and 21:1–4)

Jesus' nonviolent direct action of taking over the temple clearly shows his followers that God's kingdom asks us to reject the violent and oppressive means used to maintain the unjust status quo. We are instead invited to adopt the vision and means of Jesus. In one teaching, Jesus drew from both his divinity and his own experience of loss, lauding the sacrificing widow to provide sharp contrast with the religious officials' pretentious, spiritually vapid public offerings. The widow's profound sacrifice—mirroring Mary's—exemplifies the faith asked of us. We are to give fully to God, surrender completely to God's care, and trust in God's loving, nonviolent means for deliverance and salvation.

Widows

TODAY WE SEE JESUS at the end of his life. It seems that he has been preparing for this moment for the whole of his public ministry. Later on, we might find out that God has been preparing him for this all his life.

For three years, Jesus has been building his constituency—the poor, the hungry, the outcasts—those forgotten or banished by the state or religious authorities. Then he marches into Jerusalem—we call it "Palm Sunday" now—leading and summoning the people of his constituency, and takes over the temple, the center of Jewish worship and identity. See where it says, "He was in the temple every day teaching"?[1] And not only that, he would leave the temple at the end of every day, pray, and then return the next morning. And all the people would return daily to listen to his teaching.

Now it's easy for us who are used to praying to Jesus, to worshipping him as the Son of God, to think, "What's the problem? I mean, he's Jesus. Of course he belongs in the temple, teaching." But that ignores the historical reality of Jesus. In reality, Jesus was a day-laborer-turned-itinerant-preacher from some podunk and suspect area called Galilee. And the religious leaders of his time, believe me, did *not* think that his presence in the temple was a natural occurrence. To them it was at best an outrage, and at worst a crime against their religion and their God.

And more: they saw it as a political threat. Remember what they said as recorded in John's Gospel? "What are we going to do? . . . If we leave him alone, all will believe in him, and the Romans will come and take away both our land and our nation."[2] That was because Jesus was preaching and practicing nonviolence. And since this beginning with Jesus, that has always been the charge against nonviolence: "You can't be nonviolent. You can't be like Jesus. If we're nonviolent, then the Romans, Communists, Russians, socialists, Muslims, terrorists, Taliban, Al-Qaeda—fill in the blanks; it's a new enemy every couple of years—will come and take over our country." But in fact the leaders are not so afraid of invasion. In reality, instilling that fear into the hearts and minds of their people keeps them in power. On a deep level, they love the threat of invasion. It keeps the people obedient. No, the leaders are afraid of nonviolence, because it is a people's movement, because it is a force more powerful than the violence on which they have staked their careers and identities, and because it challenges the paradigms of fear that silence the people and hold them in positions of submission.

So, Jesus shows them a dimension of nonviolence that really challenges this model of fear instilled by the few into the many, challenges the silencing and dominance it spawns. He performs what we now call a nonviolent direct action. He takes over the temple. And today he centers his teaching on a single, simple figure: a widow who deposits two coins in the temple treasury.[3] But this is not the first time Jesus has drawn our attention to widows. They seem to be a recurrent theme in his ministry. He starts off

1. Luke 19:47.
2. John 11:47–48.
3. See Luke 21:1–4.

his chastisement of the religious leaders by castigating them: "They devour the houses of widows and, as a pretext, recite lengthy prayers."[4] And today, he says of this widow, "Look, she's given more than all the rest."[5] And earlier, remember?—when he saw the body of a young man being brought out, the only son of a widow, Jesus touched the bier and said to the widow, "Do not weep," and raised her son.[6]

Okay, so what is it with Jesus and widows? Why is he so concerned with them? Did you ever think that Jesus cared so much about widows because his own mother was a widow? Can you see the quiet rage of the young Jesus as the scribes and Pharisees came from the big city to his mother's house and ate and drank and ate and drank, consuming what little he and Mary had until they were finished with their show of prayers? How could he fail to be moved when he saw his mom give up first Joseph and then Jesus—the one to God and the other to the people—two small coins. Everything she had to live on.

You know, the Hebrew word for "widow" contains the notion of "being silenced" within it. The Jewish Law at that time did not provide for her to inherit anything from her husband. If she was also without a son, she was helpless. For Jesus, this was a source of personal pain. And that someone would even go so far as to take advantage of them—this merited his rage. And it was following that sensitivity of Jesus that the early church also focused on making sure that widows were cared for. We might even say that they were the first "order" in the Catholic Church. It was one of the chief ways they made sure that the will of God was done "on earth as it is in heaven."[7]

We have much to do to make God's kingdom of nonviolence come. We must take a stand against the violence of the death penalty that creates widows. We must oppose the massive fear-inspired violence of war that makes for widows in the tens, the hundreds of thousands. We must lend our voice to the widows, not the widow-makers.

And in all this, we are not discouraged. Because we believe in the son of a widow who was raised from the death of oppression. Because in this passage, this Son of God gives us a touchstone we can use to determine if we are following his way. The kingdom of God is a world where widows can

4. Luke 20:47.
5. Luke 21:3.
6. Luke 7:13–14.
7. Matt 6:10.

walk and can speak, confident and unafraid. And with them, all those who have been sentenced to silence by the state or by the religion.

"Oh house of Jacob, come, let us walk in the light of the Lord!"[8]

Philip's Reflection

Simon used Scripture to illuminate Jesus' nonviolent opposition to those whose ungodly actions create and exploit widows. The Jewish culture and religion of Jesus' time had strict rules that could leave widows to fend for themselves under certain circumstances. We recall that at his death, Jesus directed John to care for Mary.[9] Mary was symbolic of the widow in the parable who gave two coins, whom Jesus praised for "offering her whole livelihood,"[10] leaving her totally reliant on God's graces to sustain her—through those in the earthly kingdom of God. Jesus' disciples are to care for the widow, as we are required to care for the marginalized people whom Simon called "Jesus' constituency." These are the clearly articulated actions expected for those who follow Jesus closely: We are to immerse ourselves with those who suffer and alleviate it when possible; share our gifts with those in need; and in the words of my social justice colleagues, ally ourselves with the oppressed to empower them without condescension, or imposition of what we, the "more powerful," presume is best. Simply put, we are to act in the same ways as Jesus did with *our* poor, disenfranchised, ostracized, demonized, and misunderstood people. Each of us can ask God to help us determine how we can act to best serve God, given our circumstances and talents.

When Christians do what Jesus did and enter the lives of those on the damaging end of social inequities, including the draining of social and financial resources for the purposes of war, domination, death, and destruction, we see firsthand the deleterious effects of institutionalized violence and war. But how long would we continue to live in our vicious cycle of violence if each of the 70 percent of adult American Christians[11] chose to align themselves with Jesus' nonviolent ways and means of resisting evil and addressing conflicts? Why are Catholic laity and almost all ordained *not* following Pope Francis's clear redirection towards Jesus' nonviolent

8. Isa 2:5.

9. See John 19:27.

10. Luke 21:4.

11. "American," line 1.

means? He urged that we "make active nonviolence a way of life . . . [and reasserted that] the name of God cannot be used to justify violence."[12] Let all Catholics and Christian churches heed Archbishop Wester's historic amplification of Francis's message in January of 2022, "to understand Jesus and the Gospels in light of 'nonviolence,' as a fresh, new way to live out our discipleship in the nuclear age."[13] He further urged us to "practice and study the nonviolence of Jesus daily so that we can decrease our violence and become peacemakers."[14]

Imagine if each of the two hundred and thirty-three million US Christians committed to making that prayer and study a daily practice? Perhaps we would be moved to nonviolently oppose that which diminished and harmed people.

Jesus' courageous nonviolent direct action provided an example for his followers to take similar creative actions, many proven quite effective.[15] But nonviolent actions take the same level of intelligent planning, focus, courage, and willingness to die, as made by those who prepare for and fight wars.

Finally, we must not hold enmity in our heart towards the oppressors among us. Jesus tells us not to foment anger at others.[16] Anger can lead to violence, and violence or its threat is at the core of sustaining those institutions counter to God's kingdom. Violence is absent from the core of our loving and merciful God, and therefore should be absent from the hearts and actions of God's servants.

Questions to Consider: We live in a violent country, within a violent world. What are reasons given (and by whom) *against* employing nonviolence? What are the various threats to the existence of nation-states like ours? What are some creative, nonviolent actions that have been taken? Recall the times in the New Testament that Jesus referenced widows. What do

12. Francis, "Nonviolence," 4.

13. Wester, "Living in the Light," 13.

14. Wester, "Living in the Light," 42.

15. See Albert Einstein Institution; and Francis, "Nonviolence," 3–4, for historical examples. I urge readers to peruse the former website, founded in 1983 by Gene Sharp, a giant in nonviolent studies. Students in my peace courses were shocked to discover that people have historically enacted 198 different types of nonviolent actions. Many students were also dismayed, questioning why they had never been taught any of them, only learning of warfare.

16. See Matt 5:21–23.

you think his attitudes were towards them, based on the scriptural stories? What other people or groups could widows symbolize? Is the US government and its political leaders our ultimate authority? If we identify as followers of Christ, is he our ultimate authority?

The kingdom of God is a community where widows—and all who have been hurt by life's circumstances, or silenced and victimized by state or religious oppression—can live fulfilled, confident, and unafraid lives.

8

Why Did the Congregation Want to Kill Jesus after Hearing His First Sermon? (Luke 4:16–30)

Jesus' first sermon proclaims the fulfillment of the Hebrew Scripture's promise of a Messiah, but without the promise of God's vengeance towards adversaries. God's love and salvation is not restricted to select religious groups, regardless of their own sense of exclusivity. Congregations then and now are deeply inured to the false vision and support of a vengeful God, and reliant on the empty promises of liberation through violent and punitive force. Then, and now, people try to kill those unexpected liberatory messages by trying to silence Jesus. We explore the essential element of nonviolent love and compassion for all of God's people as foundational components to God's kingdom.

Jesus' First Sermon

TODAY WE READ OF Jesus' first sermon—and it doesn't seem to turn out well. The congregation ends up trying to kill him. Why? To start, it helps to know a bit of the historical situation. Jesus is living among a fiercely proud people, a chosen people, who have been conquered by an empire of unbelievers. Now they're under occupation—a benign occupation, a "pax Romana," but occupation nonetheless, whatever the Romans want to call it. And the Romans, for all their military might and sophistication, are

Gentiles, people who do not have the special call from the one God that the Jews have. And it was really hard for the Jews to convince themselves that their God is most high while the emperor and the gods of Rome still ruled over them with their mighty legions of soldiers and mercenaries. I remember how Herod had all those babies killed right after Jesus was born. That kind of oppression. And I know about the hundreds and hundreds of people being hung up naked on crosses for rebellion against the empire. That kind of state-sponsored terror.

The Jews responded to all this with all kinds of resistance. And one of the ways that most appealed to most of the people was that God would send an anointed one, a messiah to conquer their imperial overlords and cast those unclean Gentile legions out of their holy land. This is the world into which Jesus was born, and the atmosphere into which he enters to preach his first sermon, back in his hometown of Nazareth. When Jesus is invited to speak, he chooses a messianic passage from the prophet Isaiah—one with promises that were well known to the whole congregation. Word for word. "The Spirit of the Lord is upon me, because he has anointed me to bring glad tidings to the poor . . . to proclaim liberty to captives and recovery of sight to the blind, to let the oppressed go free, and to proclaim a year acceptable to the Lord."[1]

Even though I know how people responded at the very end of this sermon, I want to just pause a moment and reflect. What would be "glad tidings for the poor"? Would it mean just a handout, some food from a soup kitchen, a kind word? Maybe that would help a little, but how about job training and the dignity of having a job and a place to call home? How about the pride of being able to care for your children in their needs, to walk with your head up among your neighbors and friends? And how would the promise of "liberty to captives" be received? Who might hear that as good news? Let me ask a related question: What is the country that has a higher percentage of its population in the prison system than any other country on the face of the earth?[2] And good news for the oppressed? Is there a certain developed country in the world with the greatest gap between rich and poor?[3]

---

1. Luke 4:18–19.

2. See World Population Review, "Incarceration Rates," lines 3–9. Sadly, this fact has not changed in the fifteen years since Simon wrote this. The US still leads the world, with 629 people in prison per 100,000 of our population.

3. Bucholz, "Top Ten Percent," lines 1–15.

And what's this acceptable year to which the prophet and Jesus refer? It's a year when all debts are cancelled. Imagine this good news to a congregation whose livelihoods had been consumed by a combination of the oppressive rich and taxes from the empire and the religion. I remember how Jesus fed five thousand people. We almost never consider why there were so many people wandering around, following him for three days. Where were their homes? Why did they all have no jobs, no food? And at that point, Jesus rolls up the scroll and sits down, and Luke's Gospel tells us that all eyes in the synagogue were fixed upon him. Why? Because they all knew this reading by heart, and its promises word for word. And Jesus had left out a verse.

Jesus was reading from the first few verses of Isaiah, chapter 61. I want to read it along with him. "The Spirit of the Lord is upon me"—Jesus said that. "He has anointed me to bring good news to the poor"—he said that. "To proclaim liberty to captives and recovery of sight to the blind"—yep, he said that too. "To free the oppressed and announce the year acceptable to the Lord"—yes . . . "a day of vengeance for our God."[4] Wait! Jesus didn't say that. And all eyes were fixed on him, because everyone was saying to themselves, "Finish the verse! 'A day of vengeance for our God.' 'A day of vengeance for our God.' Finish the verse; call down God's vengeance on these Gentiles, these oppressors. Finish it; finish them!" But Jesus didn't read that verse. Just when everyone expected him to say it, instead he rolled up the scroll and put it away. He rolled up the scroll like the rolling of the scroll in the book of Revelation. Jesus wasn't going to read about vengeance. He is not going to call for vengeance. Not Jesus. No vengeance for him; no vengeance in the kingdom he is initiating with this first sermon of his.

Jesus verifies that this Isaiah passage is coming true at this very moment, and begins to explain how. The Scripture reports that people began grumbling at him from the first. But Jesus always gets me nervous at times like these. He just won't back off! He's already upset them with the "vengeance" omission, but then he pushes it even further. "Remember," he says, "from the Scripture when there was that great drought? Well, God didn't favor any of the 'chosen people' with Elijah's miracle. He favored a Gentile widow. And not only that, but remember from the Scripture how many lepers there must have been in the time of Elisha? Well, God didn't favor

---

4. Isa 61:1–2 (CCB; emphasis added).

any of the 'chosen people' with Elisha's healing. Only Naaman the Gentile was healed."[5]

The conclusion was all too obvious—especially to the congregation: "Sometimes, God favors the Gentiles more than God favors us. So what's this vengeance stuff about?" I wonder, Did Jesus expect the reaction he got? He must have had at least some suspicion. It wouldn't be so different now, if someone said even something relatively mild, like, "Maybe we ought to listen a bit to the folks who attacked us on September 11. Maybe they've got some points that are valid." Imagine (I really don't have to; I've tried that) what a firestorm of criticism and attacks and "patriotic fervor" that would arouse! Well, seconds later, they all storm Jesus, haul him out of town to throw him off one of the Nazareth hills to kill him. I've been to Nazareth— pretty steep hills. I remember thinking, "The boy Jesus must have gotten in pretty good shape running up and down these hills."

But then something weird happens as they're forcing Jesus to the brink: "But he passed through the midst of them and went away."[6] What happened? What's this slipping away that Jesus did? Did they get distracted somehow? Was something else on their minds? "Buy milk, get eggs, kill Jesus"?

I think that the gospel is telling us something else here. It is saying, "You can begin in church, you can begin listening reverently to the Scriptures, you can be hearing a great homily by a terrific charismatic preacher; you can even have the presence of Jesus in your midst; but as soon as you become so convinced of the rightness of your cause that you're prepared to do violence—Jesus slips away from you! He's just not there with you anymore."

I think I heard an echo of that when the Vatican wrote to the US government and George Bush right before the 2003 "shock and awe" invasion of Iraq. The Vatican said, "If you go into Iraq, you go without God." And sure enough, that godlessness has characterized our invasion and occupation and torture ever since.

If we ever intend to inaugurate Jesus' vision of the kingdom of God, it looks as though vengeance, the sense of superiority of one people over another, and violence, will just leave us wandering in a desert of despair without Jesus.

5. See 2 Kgs 5:1–19.
6. Luke 4:30.

Philip's Reflection

Jesus' kingdom is one that does not sanctify or endorse vengeance and violence as ways for liberation—or as justified means for any desired outcome. Jesus, the Word of God, offers us a new way to know, love, and serve God. But Simon's reflection reminded me of how far our kingdoms and too many Christian church practices are from Jesus' kingdom. Seventy percent of adult Americans identify as Christians,[7] and 70 percent of the US military also identify as Christians.[8] I presume many of the Christian military personnel and their families are committed, dedicated, and courageous individuals, sacrificing much in service to their values. But how many of them have been counseled by the churches, or have prayerfully considered that preparation for and committing violent actions are incompatible with Jesus' clear teachings? Why is Christ's nonviolent way of confronting evil, let alone its enactment, not even a matter of serious discussion among all of us?

Students in my peace studies and social justice courses were initially dubious about nonviolence as an effective strategy in the face of threats, often associating it with nonaction, or passivity. The word *nonviolence* even sounds like a "not-doing, the putting all of one's energy into avoiding something, rather than [the intended meaning] of throwing one's total being into doing something good."[9] Christians have told me that "turn the other cheek" is an unrealistic ideal, and even a passive acceptance of evil. Some have quoted Jesus' direction to "offer no resistance to one who is evil" as scriptural direction of acquiescence.[10] The late scholar Walter Wink helped us learn that that passage has been inadequately translated from the Greek, probably because of political motives. Human evolution conditioned us to fight or avoid, through submission or flight. Monarchs and authoritarian rulers are served when the ruled people continue to think they had only those two options. King James' "faithful scholars" rendered a translation that maintained those options, while omitting Jesus' complete meaning. Asserting the absurdity of Jesus telling his oppressed audience not to resist evil, Wink endorsed the more accurate translation of *antistēnai* to "Don't

---

7. "American," line 1.

8. Kizer and Le Menestrel, *Strengthening the Military*, 86.

9. Wink, *Jesus and Nonviolence*, 3.

10. Matt 5:39.

43

react violently against one who is evil."[11] Wink also provided historical context for Jesus' three brief examples of creative, nonviolent resistance to evil. For example, because of the customs and heavy fines incurred for its violation, standing and facing the striker by turning one's cheek was a courageous act of defiance that forced the assailant, against his will, to "regard this subordinate as an equal human being."[12]

This social justice question is entirely relevant: Who benefits, and who suffers, from Christians living unaware of the reality of Jesus' call for courageous, creative, nonviolent actions in the face of evil?

Simon's close reading of Isaiah provided a critical component in Jesus' fulfillment of the Scriptures. We also sympathize with the oppressed congregation; we imagine the anger of an occupied people desiring liberation, who under brutal military occupation live with the dehumanization, degradation, and loss of honor.

This meditation on Jesus' first sermon also warned that then and now, words spoken even in a holy building are not always aligned with Jesus. Sometimes, church authorities diverge from the truth. That deviation can be intentional, or the product of more subtle personal and culturally reinforced revisions. The Catholic Church has historically valued strict obedience to doctrine. But what are Christians to think and do when human beings change Jesus' words and teachings? Consider Just War Theory (JWT). It is something Jesus never preached or taught, yet for the past seventeen hundred years, until Pope Francis's historic reversal,[13] JWT had replaced his command to nonviolently love enemies. It is also a sham rationale, because to my knowledge, no war has ever been fought following all its tenets, which is required for a "just war." In fact, JWT demands that if a warring nation ever violated *one* of the tenets, it would need to immediately cease and lose the war. Unthinkable![14]

Although most cannot name every tenet, Christians will cite JWT as authoritative justification for engaging in legalized mass murder. Because of intergenerational endorsement, like the patriarchy Joseph faced, our "collective conscience" does not tend to go back to what Jesus actually said

11. Wink, *Jesus and Nonviolence*, 10–13.

12. Wink, *Jesus and Nonviolence*, 14–16. He similarly contextualizes Jesus' other two examples on 17–28.

13. Francis, "Nonviolence."

14. See McCarthy, *Christian Just War Theory*, for a logical, theological dismantling of the theory.

and did. There is a real danger of following only human authority and tradition, in or out of the church's walls. We need to nurture our friendship with Jesus to know more fully who he is, and is not.

Yet it is seductive to embrace violence as an effective means to protect the weak, to protect our own interests. I recall that early followers of Jesus, persecuted by the empire with varying intensity for over three hundred years, did not violently oppose their oppressors. They were following "The Way"—which was the name for early Christianity—of Jesus' nonviolent but direct resistance to evil. I imagine they took literally Jesus' commandment to love *all others* in the ways he loved people, and to know that each person housed the Holy Spirit. Harming another was literally a sacrilegious act. Loving as Jesus loved presents a stark contrast to our world, but it is the way that others "will know you are [Jesus'] disciples."[15]

Jesus' ways are sometimes quite different from what we are told, from our "common sense" infused by socialization. Jesus' first sermon also reminded us that we Christians must not act as if we are the only group God loves. If Jesus is God, my job as a disciple is not to justify negating his teachings to fit my own or authorities' worldviews. Rather, it is to pray for the grace and courage to deepen my companionship with him and to act like him. When we do so, like Jesus, we can expect harsh rebuke, even from those who also identify as his followers.

Resistance to our God's ways was foreshadowed in the desert when Jesus was tempted by Satan to save the world using Satan's means, not those of the Father. Of course, we know that Jesus continually rejected those means, even unto his excruciating execution. We should too, with the grace of God.

Jesus knows infinitely more about what courses of action will lead to total harmony, peace, and unity with God. Some of those ways, such as limitless forgiveness, returning good for evil, and loving those that disrespect or hate us, are difficult and unpopular. But I choose to trust that he—not I or any human—knows precisely the way out of the desert and into God's kingdom.

Questions to Consider: When might a person or group of people seek vengeance? When does our culture, through entertainment, or any other form of expression, validate and justify revenge? Research Walter Wink's term "The Myth of Redemptive Violence," and discuss. Has Jesus ever

15. John 13:34–35.

disappointed you? That is, have you or a group you are familiar with ever expected God/Jesus to act in a way that you *knew* was what God *should* do? What is one specific way that Jesus' kingdom differs from the kingdoms of this world? Research the tenets of JWT. Reflect upon, or discuss in groups what Jesus would say about JWT. What are the pros and cons of relying exclusively on human authorities/experts?

When we rely on violence, vengeance, the sense of superiority of one people over another to build our vision of God's kingdom, Jesus slips away.

9

What We Learn from the Syrophoenician
Woman's Great Faith (Matt 15:21–29)

*This woman, along with the Roman centurion, are the only two in
Scripture whose faith Jesus verbally commended. We learn we are to
embrace the core goodness the Creator has endowed us, and through
that awareness, prayerfully and persistently communicate with God.
Like this woman, we are to bring our authentic selves to God, to keep
reaching out, and accept that the Holy Spirit of Truth will provide us
with what we need to courageously participate with God's will. We also
learn that faith is an active, ineluctable drive towards God and the
liberation that characterizes God's kingdom.*

The Syrophoenician Woman

I THINK I CAN claim privilege over this pericope, because I really do have
powerful and even defiant women in my Lebanese family. I am Lebanese—
and the Lebanese of today are the Phoenicians of long ago. Modern ar-
chaeologists even have the DNA tests to prove it. So this is twice a family
story for me: first, because of my brother Jesus and second, because I can
claim this woman as a distant relative of mine. There's a Lebanese saying,
"Sometimes, when you need fire, you have to take it with your bare hands."
I don't see this woman as humbling herself further; it just seems out of
character. I think that she found a way to do a "faith jujitsu" so that she
could relate to Jesus as an equal—which worked, it seems to me, because

47

that's the point of the incarnation in the first place. I remember that one day, my sister drove me to the train station. I got on the train, and the train moved about one hundred feet and stopped. Then a slightly exasperated conductor got on the train and asked if there was a "Simon Harak on board." I identified myself and he told me that he had my cell phone, which I had inadvertently left on the seat of my sister's car. My sister had stopped the train. She stopped the train and compelled the conductor to give me back my phone! Well, here's some reflections from the brother of a Syrophoenician woman about his sister.

This is only one of two times in all the Gospels that Jesus verbally compliments someone on his or her faith. All the other times Jesus is criticizing people for their *lack* of faith. Once he said to the leaders, "How can you believe when you accept praise from one another and do not seek the praise that comes from the only God?"[1] And even, perhaps especially, to his apostles: "You of little faith," "Where is your faith?"[2] Or to Peter: "You of little faith, why did you doubt?"[3]

But here we have a person whom Jesus compliments on her faith: "Woman," he says to her, "great is your faith!"[4] So it's important, I think, to find out what she did to earn that prized recognition from the Son of God. And maybe, in imitating her faith we disciples can one day impress Jesus with our own. I mean, we try to imitate the other Gentile, the centurion, in his faith by repeating his words at Mass, "Lord, I am not worthy . . ."[5] So we should try to imitate this woman as well. But for sure, there's not much self-humbling with her!

I imagine the scene. Jesus has just had another run-in with the scribes and Pharisees. He's been challenging them on clean and unclean foods and he got so angry that he called them hypocrites and quoted Isaiah to them to condemn them. His apostles tried to warn him not to offend the religious leaders, but he got angrier, saying that the religious leaders were like the blind leading the blind.

Then Jesus, perhaps sensing an imminent retaliation, withdraws from Israel and goes north into Syrophoenicia, into modern Lebanon. He leaves the land of the chosen people, and withdraws into Gentile territory. And

1. John 5:44.
2. Luke 12:28; 8:25.
3. Matt 14:31.
4. Matt 15:28.
5. Matt 8:8.

here comes this woman to accost him: "Have mercy on me, Lord, Son of David; my daughter is tormented by a demon."[6]

It's important to observe something here. This woman has broken the honor code. Honor is unimaginably important to us people of the Middle East. Of course, Jesus is partly at fault himself: he's crossed the border; he's gone "over the line" as a Jew going into Gentile territory. But for the woman to approach him—that's another difficulty. First, she's a Gentile. She should know that this Jew would not even talk to her. And second, she's a Middle Eastern woman approaching a Middle Eastern man. This is not just an awkward social gaffe; it is a violation of the honor code. This woman is putting both herself and Jesus to shame by approaching him.

In the face of this violation, Jesus the Middle Eastern man has three options. He can tell his disciples, "Get rid of her," and they no doubt would, probably by throwing stones at her until she withdrew. The second is that he can try to ignore her—pretend, as it were, that the shameful thing is not happening. Westerners are perhaps a little more familiar with this approach. If we're sensitive and something socially awkward happens, we pretend it didn't happen and go on. Jesus tries this approach, as we can see: "he did not say a word in answer to her."[7]

Well, that doesn't work either. The woman is so persistent that, in a humorous reversal, the apostles come to Jesus to ask him to send her away, instead of the other way around, "for she keeps calling out to us."[8]

A note here. The apostles are constantly making this mistake. They keep asking Jesus to send people away—to send the crowds away, to send the children away, to send this woman away. And whenever they do, it seems to remind him of his promise to us: "I will not reject anyone who comes to me."[9] Not reject anyone.

So Jesus tries the third cultural option available to him. He presents the woman with her violation of the honor code and gives her an opportunity to explain why she's doing what she knows she shouldn't be doing. I recall that the woman at the well did this for Jesus when he violated the honor code by asking her for a drink. She asked, "How can you, a Jew, ask me, a Samaritan woman, for a drink?"[10]

6. Matt 15:22.
7. Matt 15:23.
8. Matt 15:24.
9. John 6:37.
10. John 4:9.

Jesus does the same thing here. He's hard-pressed to do anything else because the Gospel tells us that she has run around the group of disciples and is now kneeling at his feet. He says, "I was sent only to the lost sheep of the house of Israel." But this doesn't deter my Lebanese sister at all. "Lord, help me!" she says, probably tearfully. Then Jesus must explain the violation very strongly—perhaps she doesn't get it. "It is not right to take the food of the children," he tells her, "and throw it to the dogs."[11]

It looks as though the word for "dog" here is softer than the usual insulting term—it's more like "household pet." But it still partakes of the structure of exclusion that the religions of that time had set up: there are the chosen *people,* and the Gentile *dogs.* I have to confess, in almost any interpretation, it seems like a fairly harsh rebuke. I wonder what my Lebanese sister will do. Will she accept the rebuke and go away with her petition unanswered? Really? Then you don't know any Lebanese women! "Please Lord," she says, "for even the dogs eat the crumbs that fall from the table of their masters."[12]

What? What did she just say to the Son of God? She said to him, "Okay! But what are you doing here in Lebanon? If your own religious leaders had accepted you, then you wouldn't be here. So if I'm a dog, then *you* are the crumbs that just got pushed off the masters' tables. And I'd like my share!"

"Whoa! Woman! You have great faith! What you ask for will be done for you." Pretty resourceful, I'd say! And bold, I tell you—even while she's asking him a *favor.*

It seems to me that we can unlearn and learn something about faith from this story of Jesus and the Syrophoenician woman. Oftentimes, we think of faith as resignation, as a kind of passive surrender to the way things are, which we then call "the will of God." Then we hope that things will get better "someday," someday in the sweet by-and-by. Gosh! Do we need to unlearn that! In this story, neither the woman nor—more importantly—Jesus accepts this definition of faith. Faith is an active thing, a focused thing, a relentless, ineluctable drive toward God and the liberation that characterizes God's kingdom. Faith is the power that enables us to overcome barriers between us that others have ordained, to keep reaching out—ever more creatively—to the other, even when we've been ignored, even when we've been rebuked. Faith is—as we see here in the Jesus story—the unyielding insistence that we are all equal in the love of God.

11. Matt 15:24–26.
12. Matt 15:27.

How important such a faith is in our struggle against oppression! And its root is in the coming of our Savior. Today, we see that he crossed a barrier and in so doing encouraged this woman to cross a barrier herself. But in the largest setting, love called Jesus to cross the barrier between God and us, between the immortal and the mortal. Between Jew and Gentile, Catholic and Protestant, Christian and Muslim, black and white, men and women, oppressor and oppressed.

And his Spirit of love empowers us to do the same for one another: to love one another as he has loved us.[13]

Philip's Reflection

Simon takes us through this compelling story of a relentless woman undeterred by her social position, insistent upon receiving Jesus' healing power for her daughter. We can emulate her faithful persistence and active dialogue with God. We must also notice that Jesus crossed entrenched boundaries to be present to this enemy. His command that we love all others as he did is especially relevant in our country today, as we are awash with acceptable racism, xenophobia, and other forms of institutionalized and interpersonal animus. How can we act as our God did in our groups and circumstances, becoming conduits of the divine love to all people, across personal, familial, societal, and international boundaries?

We can begin by honestly examining our assumptions about what faith in God means for us, and how we can express it. We learn from her to look for other gifts and graces from God that differ from our expectations and wants. She was willing to look for crumbs from God, knowing that even they would be sufficient to heal her loved one. Too many times I find myself praying only for specific outcomes. Although Ignatius teaches the importance of identifying our desire in prayer, I need to open my heart, mind, and soul to appreciate how God will answer my prayers. My desires are limited by my experiences. God's desires for us are much larger.

Like her, in prayer I need to persist in bringing authentic parts of myself and my reactions to Jesus. Otherwise, resentment can build, and I can construct walls that give me the (mistaken) sense that God and I are unavailable to each other. Most importantly, if I shut myself off from God, I miss the healing power that makes me whole and connected. I want to

13. See John 13:34.

be open to the more subtle, nuanced, apparent "crumbs" from God that nourish me.

Bolstered by these praiseworthy faithful practices, what are we to do with and for others to help bring about God's kingdom? He literally *commands* us to love all others as he loved us; directs us to return good for evil; to feed and clothe the needy; to nonviolently oppose all forms of oppression and exclusions; and to practice endless forgiveness and mercy. There is no exclusion in the kingdom due to race, gender, sexual orientation, or any other socially constructed identifier of difference. Let us not participate in any way with those exclusions.

We acknowledge how challenging it is to act in opposition to culture's prescribed and accepted ways to think and act. For example, we are expected to be patriotic, defined by Webster's as "love for one's country."[14] For the Christian, what are our primary obligations if our country's officials take actions in opposition to Jesus and his kingdom? Christians may argue that we are obliged to serve the authorities, whom God must have ordained. But if we unequivocally exalt one nation above all others, we are nationalistic, and if that exaltation exceeds our primary allegiance to God, we are idolatrous.[15] No human, regardless of position, and no ideology, regardless of its reverential fanfare and mass appeal, must supplant our allegiance to Jesus and his ways.

Have we Christians still not learned the fatal consequences of the damning pledge, "We have no king but Caesar"?[16]

Early in the 1990s I stood at our weekly group's protest of our sanctions and blockade against the people of Iraq. I silently held a photograph of three Iraqi infants starving to death as a direct result of the incredibly draconian starvation policy we maintained for many years.[17] Would Jesus want me to support our sanctions because they were ordered by our government?[18] Punishing, merciless, murderous actions, regardless of anyone or any nation's justifications, is not loving in the ways he commanded.

14. *Merriam Webster's Collegiate Dictionary*, 909.

15. See *Merriam-Webster*, "Difference," for discussion of patriotism vs. nationalism.

16. John 19:15.

17. See Carlson, "Crusader," about former US Attorney General Ramsey Clark's characterization of those sanctions as genocidal. Many others were steadfastly opposed to that infanticidal policy, yet their voices remained largely muted, or ridiculed, by the mainstream media.

18. One organization that publicly and steadfastly opposed to the sanctions was created by Simon and Kathy Kelly, called Voices in the Wilderness. It defied federal laws of

As Simon and others have pointed out, it was no accident that God chose to send God's Son into a territory occupied by an empire. Within that context, we can more readily imagine Jesus' words and teachings against oppression of all kinds, and for liberation for everyone.

Questions to Consider: Consider the implications of this statement on the incarnation: Jesus became human so that we could relate to him in all ways as a fellow human being. What can we learn from the two people whose faith Jesus complimented? One of those complimented was a Roman occupier. What does Jesus' healing response and praise of his faith teach us about loving even the oppressor? Prior to this scene, why was Jesus upset with the religious leaders? What applications do his objections have for us and our religious leaders, especially considering our personal relationship with God, and discipleship within communities? What specifically does Jesus promise to anyone who comes to him? Is faith in God a kind of passive surrender? After careful self-examination, identify the challenges you faced or face in truly loving all others as Jesus loves you and all of us. Have you ever asked for something specific in prayer, and received something else? How can even the metaphoric "crumbs" from the Master's table nurture us? What might those crumbs look like?

We help build God's kingdom by choosing to rely on God's gift of faith— a faith that is an active, focused power that enables us to overcome barriers between us that others have ordained.

---

aiding and abetting the enemy by making frequent trips to Iraq to offer donated medicines, food, clothing, and toys to the children of Iraq. Each time those courageous members of the organization made their publicized trips, they faced twelve years in federal prison and one million dollars in fines. Aiding and comforting our enemies is an illegal action against our nation.

10

Jesus' Incarnation Heals Us and Empowers Us to Ministry (Mark 7:31–37)

By closely examining Jesus' healing of the deaf person, we discover that Jesus not only cures maladies but restores our full humanness. Jesus' immersion into our humanity completely validates it and closely connects us to him. This healing again demonstrates that God's kingdom includes everyone. Builders of that kingdom are invited to participate in those healing powers. Disciples are especially asked to offer Christlike presence to those separated literally and figuratively by illness, disability, marginalization, poverty, and other burdens.

On Jesus' Healing in the Decapolis

IN THIS PASSAGE JESUS once again heals the sick: this is Jesus as we've always seen him. Jesus does not counsel the sick person, "This is your cross, and God wants you to bear it." Never does Jesus say this to a sick person who approaches him. And since Jesus doesn't say this about sickness, we disciples shouldn't say it, either.

But there's something unusual about this particular healing nevertheless. I think it's the sheer physicality. Just recently, I was held in the hospital for a few days for observation. Everything was so clean and antiseptic. The doctors, nurses, and even the aides wore those thin gloves on their hands. That's good, I know. Ever since at least Louis Pasteur we know that disease can be conveyed from human to human if we're not careful. At the same time, it's isolating. You're there with your sickness, the only messy one in the room. Everyone else is so clean and healthy. Sometimes, during all this, you feel not only sick, but in a very basic way, unclean.

I think that this guy felt that way in today's reading. Deaf in a world of those who can hear. Stammering or perhaps even mute in a world of those who can speak. Isolated. Profoundly alone. Messy, maybe. Maybe even unclean.

Then Jesus begins the transformation of this man's reality. First, he takes the man off by himself. It's as though he is compelling the man to face his isolation—but not alone this time. This time, Jesus is with him. Then, as they stand apart together, Jesus does something that perhaps makes us raise our eyebrows a bit. He doesn't just heal with a word or by the warm laying on of hands the way he usually does. No, Jesus sticks his fingers right in this guy's ears. Then he spits. He spits! And then he touches the guy's tongue. Nothing antiseptic here, for sure. What is Jesus doing, for heaven's sake?

A strange thing about bodies. As Christians we know that bodies are sacred. But we also know that bodies can get pretty messy. And if we're not careful, we can equate being messy with being unclean, unholy. Well, we can learn something from moms and dads, I guess. I mean, look at the way they are with babies. Giving birth, changing diapers, blowing their noses, feeding them by spooning the food off their face and back into their mouths—parents know that bodies can be messy but still precious, still sacred.

It looks as though Jesus knows that, too. And something more. Jesus heals this man not by standing apart, a member of a sterile world. This healing shows that Jesus is not afraid to get messy himself—not afraid to join this sick person in his isolation and uncleanness. He can take that risk because he is relying on the Holy Spirit within him. The same Holy Spirit by which Jesus was conceived in his mother's womb, by which he healed and worked his miracles—the same Holy Spirit who would lift Jesus from the shame, from the curse of death on a cross. In a sense, this healing is a recapitulation of his incarnation. Jesus is not afraid to join us in the messiness of our bodies. Through his risk of taking on this human flesh, we humans are healed, saved, and made sacred.

There's another thing I can see for us to learn from Jesus in this healing. Look at where Jesus is. He's in Gentile territory. He's healing a Gentile. And you know, from the perspective of the Jewish people, the Gentiles are people to keep away from, to keep isolated—people who were unclean.

Evidently not for Jesus. He has no problem associating with people that holy people think of as unclean. In fact, he's unafraid to touch them.

What about us? How should we live out our belief that we too are healed, are saved, are made holy by Jesus—that as the body of Christ, we must act as he did in our world? "This is the way we may know we are in union with him: whoever claims to abide in him ought to live [just] as he lived."[1]

Are there people I still think of as unclean—as people I should hold at arm's length, people I am told we should keep apart from? The list that's presented to me as a twenty-first century American is long enough: What about gays and lesbians, bisexual or transgender individuals? What about Muslim or Christian fundamentalists? What about those people who believe in the death penalty, in war, or violence? Are we afraid to associate with those folks, afraid to get messy or to "catch" their so-called "illness"?

Not if we are rooted in prayer. Not if we keep ourselves always in the company of Jesus. Not if we are filled with his Spirit. In fact, in finding the outcast, the isolated, the messy people, we find Jesus. Because these are the people he came to save—these are the people with whom Jesus identified. And when we find Jesus, we find our salvation because "For our sake he made him to be sin who knew no sin, so that we might become the righteousness of God in him."[2]

Philip's Reflection

Simon told me that Mark was a favorite Gospel writer. He liked his brevity, and like good poetry, much is communicated in an economy of words. Here again we see Jesus showing us specific ways to enact his kingdom.

Simon suggested that we should do as Jesus did in addressing the sick. As this man was an enemy of the Jews, Jesus is also teaching us to minister to enemies as well. Walter Wink asserted that "love of enemies [is] the litmus test of authentic Christian faith . . . [T]he ultimate religious question today is . . . 'How can I find God in my enemy?'"[3] Pope Benedict called Jesus' command to love our enemies the "*magna carta* of Christian nonviolence." He further asserted that "[l]ove of one's enemy constitutes the nucleus of the 'Christian revolution,' a revolution not based on strategies

1. 1 John 2:5–6.
2. 2 Cor 5:21.
3. Wink, *Jesus and Nonviolence*, 58–59.

of economic, political, or media power: the revolution of love, a love that does not rely ultimately on human resources but is a gift of God which is obtained by trusting solely and unreservedly in his merciful goodness."[4] What is incomprehensible is how we who follow Christ can prepare to kill, and kill our enemies, while loving them at the same time.

Along with formally designated enemies of the United States, an enemy can be anyone, even friends and family, who obstruct us from meeting our interests. Jesus' outreach and healing of Gentiles is our invitation to go beyond our own like-groups and act in responsive love to conservatives, liberals, Republicans, Democrats, white supremacists, Muslims, atheists, and all others who look or believe differently than we do. We need not endorse beliefs counter to God's kingdom. Rather, we ask the Holy Spirit to guide us, listen to those with opposing views, and pray for the grace to see a person within any group as God's beloved. Nonviolence is not passivity, but actively seeking to honor the person's humanity, and employing the power of Christ-like love and compassion.

The Trinity counts on us to creatively use our gifts in acting responsively to all others. Conversely, our companionship with Jesus should immediately alert us that something is wrong when we are encouraged or authorized by the state, by public opinion, or personal enmity, to act or be co-opted to act in violence, in dehumanizing or demonizing the "unclean," or even in ignoring them. Jesus' miraculous healing reminds us to leave our own comfort zone, to walk among the sick and our enemies without fear, to engage with them—all while rooted in the Spirit. When we act in those ways from our own unique place in life, we become more complete by channeling God's healing love. We participate more fully in God's power. A conduit of divine grace, our soul also benefits through the enriching love. We become more complete; our loving becomes more like God's.

Perhaps becoming more God-like in love is what Jesus meant when he urged us to be perfect, as his heavenly Father is perfect.[5]

---

4. Benedict, "Angelus," lines 14; 18–19.

5. See Matt 5:48. I have grappled with Jesus' meanings and intentions of the word "perfect." How could I ever be perfect? I found that the Greek word for perfect was *teleios*, which can be translated as "perfect," but can also mean "coming to maturity, or wholeness." The latter meanings serve my suggestion that when we do what Jesus did, regardless of the personal, cultural, or religious opposition today, we become more like God. Therefore, more whole, and yes, more perfect.

Questions to Consider: What are some of the ways you have interpreted the phrase "your cross to bear"? Often when one is sick, they feel isolated. What is Jesus' response to those who are sick and or isolated? What specific ways can we use to follow the Master's example in relating to those who are isolated? Which people today are considered unclean, and should be shunned, isolated, or worse, have sanctioned physical harm done to them? What would Jesus say and do for those same people, if he were incarnate today? Who or what helps us act as Jesus would act to those "unclean" or enemies, and who or what hinders us?

We help build God's kingdom on earth by acting as Jesus did in relying on the Holy Spirit to help us to be fully present and responsive to those isolated and in need.

11

How We Can Return to God's Kingdom
(Matt 13:31–33)

Jesus likened God's kingdom to tiny mustard seeds and yeast. Like their transformation, apparently small acts of love and mercy grow to magnificent life-enriching proportions. We apply Gandhi's redemptive counsel to a child killer to examine the theological truths and salvific, restorative, and healing powers of Christ-like nonviolent, agape love.

The Mustard Seed and the Yeast

AT OUR MARQUETTE UNIVERSITY Center for Peacemaking,[1] we have a student group. We decided to show the movie *Gandhi*, with Ben Kingsley in the title role, in two installments with each part followed by a discussion. In the second half of the film, Gandhi travels to New Delhi, where there is intense fighting and immense bloodshed between Hindus and Muslims. A Hindu, Gandhi moves into a Muslim's home and undertakes a total fast with a fierce ultimatum: either the terrible interreligious violence stops altogether, or Gandhi will continue his fast until he dies. The struggle, non-violence against violence, goes on and on.

---

1. See Marquette University Center for Peacemaking. Late in 2006, Terry and Sally Rynne proposed to Marquette University an academic center to research and teach peacemaking. With the Center cofounded by Michael Duffey, Simon was the founding director, serving from its opening in January, 2008, until the illness stopped him early in 2013.

Toward the end, a truly inspiring encounter takes place. A Hindu man comes up to the rooftop porch where Gandhi is lying in bed, fighting unto death. "Eat!" The man cries to Gandhi as he flings some bread onto Gandhi's bed. "I am going to hell, but not with your death on my conscience!" Gandhi reminds the man that only God decides who goes to hell. But the man refuses any comfort. Because, he confesses, "I took a little boy" [and he puts his hand out to measure an imaginary four-foot-high child], "and smashed his head against a wall. I killed a little boy!"

At that point, I stopped the DVD. I turned to our little band and said, "What does Gandhi do next?" There is some confusion among the students at this question, but I want to urge them to think nonviolently. They're not sure, so I get more specific: "What question does Gandhi ask—what question should you ask if you're nonviolent?"

They don't know. Even after several attempts, they can't get to it. So I restart the video and Kingsley's Gandhi closes his eyes for a moment, and then asks, "Why?"

I'm remembering that scene because in all the reporting I've read and heard about the terrible violence in Mumbai, in Baghdad, in Afghanistan, at the Twin Towers in New York, but in all the radio I've heard, I've not heard anyone seriously ask, let alone pursue, why people are doing this violence. And I wonder why we don't ask, "Why?"

I think it's because we think we already know why people do violence, so we don't need to ask. It's because "Those people' don't value human life in that part of the world." It's because "Those people have a crazy religion that teaches them to be violent." And, "Hasn't there *always* been violence over there?" Or worst of all, we think that violence toward one another is, fundamentally, a characteristic of how human beings act toward each other. Just another human trait—newsworthy when it gets big or brutal enough, but otherwise nothing to wonder at, nothing to question, nothing to challenge with "Why?"

I hear that theory often when I talk with people who believe in war. "Well, there are always going to be wars," they say, as though war is a cosmic reality that descends upon us from time to time, or is a natural human function instead of what it truly is: a horrifying activity chosen by the will of people.

At the Center for Peacemaking, we have done work with veterans who struggle with post-traumatic stress disorder. The latest figures show that vets returning from Iraq and Afghanistan are committing suicide at the rate of 120 a *week*.[2] For me, this is just another indication that violence is not natural for us humans; instead, it disfigures and deforms our humanity. War brings a wounding for which parades are out of place, and for which healing instead is required.

When we say to violence "Why?" we undertake a new pathway of thought—a nonviolent way of thinking that does *not* consider violence to be a natural human activity. A way of thinking that demands that violence give an account of itself so that it can yield to healing and restoration.

It goes without saying that when we do that we are thinking with Jesus. I remember in the Gospel of John, when one of the high priest's guards struck Jesus. Jesus said, "If I have spoken wrongly, testify to the wrong; but if I have spoken rightly, why did you strike me?"[3] Why? asks Jesus. Why did you do this violence? Why have you done this strange, inhuman thing? What happened to you that you have turned from the humanity I gave you to this violence that is foreign to us? Remember, he speaks as one who shares our humanity fully!

Gandhi gets his answer from the Hindu man. The Muslims have killed *his* son, and in the self-justifying madness of violence he retaliated against an innocent Muslim child. Then Gandhi uses the man's answer to suggest "a way out of hell." Stretching out his hand to measure an imaginary four-foot-high child, he tells the man to find a young boy, one who, Gandhi continues, has been orphaned by violence. And then Gandhi points to the conclusion of the journey from hope to redemption for the Hindu. "But make sure he is a Muslim. And that you raise him as one."

The Hindu is stunned at first. He can't accept it. The ones who killed his own son? To support them? Even to further their life? To love his enemy? He begins to leave. But then he turns back and falls weeping upon Gandhi's bed. Arun Gandhi, Gandhi's grandson, told me that what Gandhi advised the man was exactly what he went and did, and that he and his family—Hindu and Muslim—lived a life of love and joy together.

The healing journey began with a short question: Why? But it is a question with unquantifiable philosophy, theology, and hope behind it. It ended with the salvation of peacefulness. For me, that question, "Why," spoken to the heart of the violent, is the sign of hope that Jesus speaks of today, that small, irrepressible mustard seed, that pinch of yeast that points

---

2. See Steinhauer, "Suicides among," for more current statistics.
3. John 18:23.

the way from the barrenness of our death and death-dealing, to the warmth
and nourishment of the reign of peace.

Philip's Reflection

Like many others, Simon and I were deeply affected by Richard Attenbor-
ough's 1982 Oscar-winning film, *Gandhi*. Educators and peacemakers, we
both sought to use the film in effective ways in our courses and peace work.
For issues as big as violence, we need to step through its false attribution
to "common sense"—as in, "Everyone knows that humans are naturally
violent animals"—and interrogate the origins and legitimacy of what appears to be, but is not necessarily normal or instinctual. Violence is aber-
rant behavior that counters our natural state.[4] We can invite God to bring
the power of the resurrection to heal all damage done to others and self
through the disintegrative and destructive forces of violence.

Wracked with grief and rage at the Muslim who killed his own child,
this father reacted out of the spirit of death, succumbing to the false but
enticing promises of violence: Violence will right the wrong or even the
score; it will ease our pain while punishing the transgressor; it will make its
agent feel better. Who, in honest self-reflection, has found those promises
to be true when having acted or spoken violently?

One observation emerges: what seems like a small act, like finding
a grain of compassion, of mercy, and nurturing it, will enable us, like the
Hindu man who bravely accepted Gandhi's challenge, to more fully engage
in the all-powerful healing force of love that describes but does not con-
tain our God. That love cannot include the disintegration and harm that
violence causes. As we nurture our friendship and our journey with Jesus,
we come to know that forgiveness, compassion, and love are the commerce
within his kingdom.

Questions to Consider: Have you ever sought to understand the reasons
why people use violence? If so, list and briefly explain as many reasons as
you can. Is violence a natural way of acting for us? If yeast and mustard
seeds are the symbolic "tiny components" of compassion, forgiveness, and
love, what can those components of God's kingdom produce? What are the

---

4. See Adams, "Seville," for one of a growing body of literature to support that
statement.

causes and effects of vengeance? When we commit wrongdoing, what are ways we can make amends?

No sin, regardless of its rationale or results, is too great to separate us from God's love and welcoming into the kingdom. Expiation for some sins means restoring life for those similarly harmed.

12

All Live Life in Its Fullness in God's Kingdom (Matt 20:1–17)

We explore again the wondrous generosity within God's kingdom. When we appreciate in our mind, heart, and soul that our own salvation is a free and eternally life-giving gift, we may be moved to act towards others more generously . . . like the landowner in this parable.

The Workers in the Vineyard

IN THIS PASSAGE, OUR Lord tells us an interesting, and perhaps somewhat disturbing, parable about the kingdom of heaven. A certain landowner hires men to work in his vineyard. He does this periodically all day long. Then at the end of the day's work, he pays everyone the same day's wage.

It's somewhat disturbing because it's hard not to sympathize with the ones who had worked all day being paid the same as the ones who had only worked an hour. They complain, but the landowner will have none of it. What's going on? What is Jesus trying to tell us?

Well, one thing is that Scripture scholars say that Matthew was writing in a church with both Jews and Gentiles in it. The Jews had been faithful to God the Father of our Lord Jesus Christ for generations and generations, even hundreds and hundreds of years. And then when the Johnny-come-lately Gentiles entered the church, they were given the same Spirit, could claim the same adoption as daughters and sons, had the same rights and responsibilities in the church as did the Jews. Maybe, too, the Gentiles were feeling a bit unworthy and ecclesiastically shy about stepping into their new roles in the new life.

So, Matthew had to remember a story that Jesus had told in order to draw the church's attention to what Jesus was thinking about all this. The message here is a wonderful one: that salvation is a free gift. That as much as it appears as though we've "worked" for it, it's really a grace—the word simply means "thank you"—a free gift from God.

There's an insight with a touch of humor here, too, if we look at the personality of the landowner. It appears he just wants to give away his money and is looking for any excuse to do so. Sure, the vineyard needs tending, but he seems more concerned about watching over the workers than about overseeing the vineyard. Taking care of the people more than the product. Especially the poorer workers. And that leads us into another insight, I believe, about Jesus and his family in Palestine. Let's look again at these workers.

I'm pretty familiar with unskilled workers—day laborers. It's a chancy life. You need the money to support your family, but you have almost no marketable skills except your hands and your strength. You go out to where the other workers are, and you stand and wait for a manager to come and look for workers. He comes in his pickup truck, maybe, and he's looking for young, strong workers—people who can work hard all day in the hot sun for a flat rate.

You wait there, and some days a lot of trucks come. Some days not. And when that first truck comes, things get a little hectic. You've got to push yourself to the front, show the manager just how strong and willing you are. You shout, you bluster, maybe you plead. You've got to get that paying job. But there are at least five, maybe twenty others who want it. Then the manager picks the youngest and strongest, and the truck leaves. Leaves you.

Now what do you do? You need the money to feed and care for your family. Maybe another truck will come later. Maybe it does. Then you start all over again, trying to stand out among the others.

And still you don't get chosen. Why not? Maybe you're not strong enough. Maybe all those days and days working in the field have made you look tired, weakened you. Maybe you were injured on the last job. You try to hide it, but word gets around fast—and if the manager doesn't know it, the other workers will be quick to point it out so that they can be hired.

Maybe you've just gotten too old. And, "Thanks very much for the work you've done for us in the past, but we've got a lot of work to get done now, today. You understand."

Can we take a moment to feel how it feels not to have been chosen? Frustration, shame, abandonment. Maybe even anger. But what can you do? What can you do but wait—and hope against hope? Now think about this: how do you go back to your wife, to your children, and tell them? What would you say? What would *they* say? Can you ask for understanding and compassion from a child that is crying with hunger?

No. You don't go home, not yet. You wait and wait even when you know there's no one else coming to hire. Only then do you take your shame home, when there's nothing else to do, nowhere else to go. Or are you tempted instead not to go home at all? Or try some questionable or criminal activity to take away the shame of going home penniless?

Jesus knew all about this. I hear the deep poignancy of the exchange between the landowner and those who had been waiting all day and had not gone home: "Why are you standing here idle all day?" *Because we were too weak! Because we were too sick! Because we got too old! Because everyone has forgotten us! Because no one thought we were worth anything!*

"Because no one has hired us."[1]

The folks who know Greek tell us that the job description for Joseph, Jesus' father on earth, was "*technê.*" We kind of romanticize it to mean "carpenter." But really, it doesn't mean that. It just meant "someone who worked with his hands." Maybe carpentry, yes. But maybe also masonry. Or removing stones from a field to be plowed. Or laying stones to make a fence in a field. Or maybe working in a vineyard. An unskilled day laborer. Economically, it meant, "Someone who was an illness or injury away from homelessness." For our story today, it means that Joseph was probably one of those unskilled day laborers we've been talking about. And Jesus had to watch him come back every day, a little more tired, a little more weakened, a little less young. A little less hirable.

So, Jesus took this life experience of his, and said, "What would the kingdom of God be like? It would be some place where folks like my dad got cared for even when they became weak or injured or old. And my Father in heaven, to whom all the earth and sky and sea belong, would make sure that no one ever felt left out; no one ever felt unwanted. No one ever felt unworthy."

1. Matt 20:7.

Now this parable makes sense. Because it's not so much about land-owners and workers and days wages, as it is about *family*. Specifically, Jesus' family. And hopefully, the family we call church, the family we call "the kingdom of God."

Every day we who are the inheritors of the kingdom of God say, "Your kingdom come!" We pray, "Your will be done on earth [just] as it is in heaven."[2] So let us look into our own hearts first. Do we buy goods that are cheap, without considering the burden of the labor? Do we boast about our bargains, instead of working for the dignity of all our workers? Do we tolerate and even support wars for resources, rather than support the nonviolent struggle for liberation? Do we value the accuracy of our missiles above the agonies of our sisters and brothers?

Today, let me resolve to work together—with landowners and labor-ers—for fair trade and fair wages and for dignity for all workers.

Philip's Reflection

While I was studying for my doctorate in social justice education, I read many texts about justice and fairness from a variety of specialty fields, studying parts of labor law, sociology, social psychology, criminal justice, education, history, and religion. Although each of these fields asserts or im-plies what is just and right, and can inform us, we each have our own sense of fairness. Perhaps that sense develops most feverishly during adolescence. At least, that is my unscientific observation after working with adolescents for over forty years! If we look only on the surface of this parable, even if informed by an expert source from any of the above fields, the landowner was unfair to the workers who labored all day long. I can relate on a smaller scale. In my former profession, I recall feeling jealousy for those teachers who were allowed a fast track towards licensing, finishing in less than a year, where it took me several. But Simon reminds us, using imaginative, prayerful immersion in the scene, that the kingdom of heaven is not limited by our own perspectives or experiences, or by propositions made by human experts.

The kingdom of God is much more generous, thoughtful, inclusive, and compassionate than our exclusively human attempts of formal social structures—especially those structures that have and maintain power and

2. Matt 6:10.

wealth inequities. Imagine if this parable's landowner were the ruler of an entire country, and invited or required their subjects to act the same.

Simon reminds us of a practice that Jesus repeated throughout his ministry. Jesus was a most keen observer of life and relationships around him, and he used the commonly seen and infused it with divine truths to help us see, then participate in, his new kingdom. Many can relate to Joseph and Jesus' struggles around working without insurance, sick days, job security, retirement benefits, and the like. Why it is that God decided to become someone one step from homelessness? Even more, at the end of Matthew's Gospel, God identifies with social outcasts such as the homeless.[3] Simon would often say that when you want to meet Jesus, be with those identified in that chapter. As his body on earth, what are our obligations to those most needy, most vilified? Matthew tells us that we are not to ignore the hungry or homeless, and says nothing of their culpability in their plight. We are required to welcome strangers, with no condition on the legality of their immigration status. We are not called to visit only the innocent in prison.

The landowner of this parable, God, oversees a compassionate kingdom where all are family. Counter to today's entrenched divisions, even among Christians, in God's kingdom there is no "us vs. them," only "us." Considering the goodness of this radically different kingdom, how can I use my life to help create it, as we pray in the Our Father? Am I perpetuating our kingdoms by not concerning myself with fair labor practices?

My last thought speaks to my visceral reaction to Simon reminding us that our salvation is a free gift, a grace that we do not earn. He often reminded me and others that God was "hopelessly in love" with us; there was nothing we could do or not do that would lessen or extinguish that love. I often need to sit with that in prayer, and allow that grace and reality to wash over me. For a variety of reasons, I have had difficulty in fully accepting that generosity. But when I reach in to the Holy Spirit, I receive the love and grace that surrounds the Trinity, and that felt sense helps me to act more generously to myself and all others.

Questions to Consider: What does this parable suggest about the commonly held concept of "fairness" and God's kingdom? Imagine you are each one of the vineyard workers. How would you feel when it came time to be paid? What might Jesus have observed in his life that may have served as the model for those workers? What are some current applications of this

---

3. See Matt 25:31–46.

parable of generosity and fairness to workers? Must we *earn* God's generosity? Offer possible answers to the question of why it is that God decided to become a person one step from homelessness. As members of the body of Christ, what are our obligations to those most vilified, most needy? Contemplate and discuss this paradox: In the Our Father, we pray for God's kingdom to come here, as it is in heaven . . . but Jesus tells Pilate "My kingdom does not belong to this world."[4]

In God' kingdom, each member is given a wonderful gift: We are all part of God's family where each is treated with boundless generosity and loving care.

4. John 18:36.

13

How Friends of Jesus Grieve Dying and Death (John 11:1–44)

Through words and actions, Jesus teaches his followers how to work through the long struggle with grief and death, and in the process help build his kingdom. Jesus asks us to persevere with even more faith— that ineluctable movement towards union with God—when faced with the barriers of illness and mortality. In times of crisis, in times of loss, Jesus is asking us to be patient. We are to wait and trust that he will always act in love for us, even when he doesn't seem to answer our prayers.

Jesus and Lazarus

TODAY'S STORY ABOUT JESUS and Martha, Mary, and Lazarus is one of the longest in the Gospels. I think this is so because the process of grief is so long. Because that's what this story is, it seems to me: a story of Christian grief—about how the friends of Jesus grieve.

First, we're reintroduced to the family, and told quite concretely how profound their love for Jesus is, and his for them. And we hear that they've sent a message to Jesus: "Master, the man you love is ill." We can see this as a prayer. They address Jesus very much the way Jesus tells us to address the Father: briefly, because God knows everything we need. All they have to say is, "Master, the one you love is ill."[1]

---

1. John 11:3.

Jesus responds with great faith—that all this will end well, and that people will glorify God because of it. And even more, that the family who loves him so much will help him through this difficult time. Think of that: he's really counting on them, through this crisis, to "come through" for him and help him in his mission to save the world from the fear of death. To keep thinking of him and of his mission to the world, even in the midst of this terrible personal, family crisis.

But now the Scripture tells us something that might at first sound strange. We hear of course, that Jesus loved this family, *and so* when he heard that Lazarus was sick, he stayed where he was for two days. He loved them, and so he waited. How are we to understand this? Let the Gospel tell us.

Then on the third day—do you get it?—on the third day, Jesus announces to his disciples that he's going to Judea. They must have thought that that's why he was waiting, that he was scared to go back. In fact, that's what they say to him: "Why are you going back? They'll kill you there!" But Jesus came "[to] free those who, through fear of death, had been subject to slavery all their life."[2] So he brings the "light of Life"[3] to Judea, to the family he loves.

And when he gets there, there's a whole crowd of people—this is very Middle Eastern—who are there to comfort Martha and Mary, because Lazarus has already died. But let's focus on the family. Martha hears that Jesus has come and, typical of her, goes into action right away. She rushes out to meet him and says, "Lord, if you had been here, my brother would not have died."[4] What's she saying? What would *you* say? I'll tell you what I think. I think she's saying, "Where *were* you? Didn't you get my note? Didn't you hear my prayer? I *asked* you. I prayed with great trust; I asked you to save him from death and you didn't. You didn't come. If you had come, if you were here, he wouldn't have died. *Where were you?*"

Doesn't this sound familiar to all of us who believe and have suffered any kind of loss—especially the loss of a loved one? Isn't that our first question? Where was God, we ask ourselves. We prayed and where was he? Did he not hear? When my brother was sick and then he died, when my father was sick and then he died, when my daughter was sick and then she died,

2. Heb 2:15.
3. John 8:12.
4. John 11:21.

when my husband died, when my mother died, when my wife died, God—where were you?

But Martha does not grieve, as Paul teaches us, as those who have no hope. "Even now," she says, that even after you had disappointed me, "I know that whatever you ask of God, God will give you." Jesus responds immediately, "Your brother will rise." And thank God for Martha, and her familiarity with Jesus, her trust of him. She says exactly what's in her heart. "I *know* he'll rise again, at the resurrection on the last day."[5] I know my catechism Lord, but I tell you, it's small comfort to me now. Yes, I know about the resurrection. But the last day? The last day is far off, Lord. My brother is gone *now*. I miss him now. I want to see him again now. I can't wait for this "last day"!

Now Jesus shifts tone entirely. And here's the center: "Martha," he says to her, "I am the resurrection and the life. Whoever believes in me, even if he dies, will live, and everyone who believes in me will never die. Do you believe this?"[6]

Now wait a minute! Jesus just disappointed Martha. Disappointed her greatly. And now he's asking her for *more* faith? This makes no sense—unless you're a disciple of Jesus. What Jesus asks for, in dark and difficult times, times when our faith is failing, is more faith. And if we love him, we will answer with an affirmation, as Martha did: "Yes, Lord, I have come to believe that you are the Messiah, the son of God, the one who is coming into the world."[7]

Two things to note here, please. First, Martha doesn't exactly answer Jesus' question directly. She just says what she *can* believe, what she has believed about him, and that seems to be enough for him. And second, note that Jesus talks about two levels of faith in himself. On the first level, we believe in Jesus. Then we die, and we will live again. On the second level, we *live* and believe in Jesus. Then we never die. Never die? Never die. "Do you believe this?"[8]

Now Martha goes to get her sister Mary. You remember her, the contemplative one, the one who sat at Jesus' feet, the more prayerful, reflective one. The one who really understands Jesus. Of course, she'll accept Jesus unquestioningly. Mary comes up to Jesus and she throws herself at his feet

5. John 11:21–24, emphasis added.
6. John 11:25–27.
7. John 11:27.
8. John 11:26.

and *she* says . . . "Lord if you had been here, my brother would not have died."[9] I guess it doesn't make much difference, yes? Whether you're a Martha or a Mary, you still have that same challenge for Jesus in the face of this kind of loss.

And now we hear how Jesus himself begins to grieve. He is deeply moved by the grief of those he loves. "When Jesus saw her weeping and the Jews who had come with her weeping, he became perturbed and deeply troubled. 'Where have you laid him?'" When they said, "Sir, come and see . . . Jesus wept."[10]

I need to ask you, please, to pay attention to these two powerful words: Jesus wept. Who can imagine a God weeping? And more than that, who can imagine a God weeping out of compassion for his people? Wouldn't we rather expect God to upbraid them, saying, "Where is your faith? Be strong! Believe in the resurrection." But no. Jesus wept. He wept not only because his friend Lazarus was dead. He wept because he was so saddened to see the people he loved weeping and grieving. Jesus wept for them, too.

Now oftentimes we fail to see this dimension of faith. We fall victim to this saying, "If you really believed in the teaching of Jesus, you wouldn't weep." Or perhaps, "Death is a natural part of life; why are you grieving?" Or maybe, "Don't cry; you have to be strong for the family." Some of us even might remember watching Jacqueline Kennedy stand tearlessly throughout the terrible ordeal of her husband's wake and burial service. But thank God we don't have to follow any culture's "proper principles for proper grieving." We have to follow Jesus. He had faith—enough faith to raise Lazarus from the dead. He had strength—strength enough to bear the sin of the world. And Jesus wept.

Now for the third and last time, John's Gospel reminds us of the theme. The crowd now says, "could not [h]e . . . have done something so that [Lazarus] would not have died?"[11] Martha, then Mary, and now the crowd: Where were you? Why didn't you come? Why didn't you prevent this?

Now another almost humorous exchange between Jesus and his dear friend Martha. Jesus tells the people to take away the stone that covers the tomb of Lazarus. And Martha warns him, "Lord, by now there will be a

9. John 11:32.

10. John 11:33–35.

11. John 11: 37.

stench; he has been dead four days."[12] Please notice how true to character she remains; she doesn't feel that she has to be anyone else but herself with Jesus. Jesus also draws on her relationship to him: "Did I not tell you," he says, "that if you believe you will see the glory of God?"[13] Now here in our culture, we say, "Seeing is believing." But that's not the way of true faith. Jesus tells Martha that believing is seeing: "Did I not tell you that if you believe, you will see . . . ?"[14]

And then Jesus does what he asks us to do. He prays to the Father. And he prays out loud for the sake of those who wonder out loud about the depth of his love of his disciples and friends. And from within the power of this prayer of faith, Jesus raises Lazarus from the dead. "Lazarus, come out!"[15] And the one who was dead, rises from the dead.

Then Jesus says, "Untie him, and let him go."[16] Now you know how sacred the body is in our faith. And yet we must acknowledge that this body will not be the resurrected body. For "flesh and blood cannot inherit the kingdom of God,"[17] as Paul teaches. Eventually this body will decay and make way for the new body that God has in store for us, a spiritual body. Therefore, in a sense, this body we wear now—this body is the grave clothes that must one day be taken off, so that we can put on the new human. As Paul says, "For we know that if our earthly dwelling, a tent, should be destroyed, we have a building from God, a dwelling not made with hands, eternal in heaven."[18] That is what Jesus does for Lazarus, and that is what Jesus will do for us, and for those we love.

At the end, we come back to the same question. Why did Jesus wait so long? I think this: What his friends wanted from Jesus was too small for his love. They wanted a healing. He wanted resurrection from the dead. In times of crisis, in times of loss, Jesus is asking us to wait, to trust that he will always act in love for us, even when he doesn't seem to answer the prayers *we* want answered.

He assures us that we don't have to wait until the last day to see our loved ones live. He is the resurrection and the life. All who have died are

12. John 11: 39.
13. John 11:40.
14. John 11:40.
15. John 11:43.
16. John 11:44.
17. 1 Cor 15:50.
18. 2 Cor 5:1.

alive in him who is our life. So that "whether we live or die, we are the Lord's."[19]

Do you believe this?

Philip's Reflection

Simon's words on Christian grieving are especially poignant during my own extended grief from his long illness and death. He reminds me, and all grieving people, that Jesus is encouraging us to believe, to trust in him, even when it seems like Jesus was not there when we needed him. Here, in this lengthy story of a family's grief and Jesus' impossible power, Simon uses the Scripture to underscore the authenticity and humanness of Mary and Martha and their deeply personal relationship with Jesus. Like them, we should go to God as we are, especially at critical times of searing pain and loss, and Jesus will console and work within our personality and our relationship with him. He will be there for us even if we have not spoken to him for a long time. But we tend to act in crisis in ways consistent with how we live each moment. So, if we intentionally keep company with Jesus as often as possible, during critical times, we do not have to place a "long distance" call to an unfamiliar friend.

Crises present us with a faith paradox: God is with us, although we may feel the opposite. Even through terrible family loss—or perhaps because of it—when we stagger through the grieving process, grasping onto Jesus, sometimes letting go, we hope that we will be healed. But how is it possible that our grieving walk with Jesus will help others through *their* loss and fear of death? Perhaps as probable as a God who weeps with compassion for our pain.

This miracle illustrates that our cries to him are handled in a way that reflects God's enormous love for us. Jesus' tears reveal his compassion and sustaining graces. Our God validates the depths of our despair. We can eschew platitudinous comments like "She is in a better place"; or worse, the accusatory "How could you be so sad if you believe in God?" Jesus shows us, by his immersion into our humanity, that it is entirely appropriate to be very sad. Martha's and Mary's authentic dialogues with Jesus suggest that it's understandable that we even question God's responsiveness to our suffering. Although God validates our pain, we should not fall into the temptation to believe that our grief is *all* of reality.

19. Rom 14:8.

Grief can be a life-shattering experience that takes time to heal from. Throughout the entire process, as much as possible, we need to continue to call on the Trinity and to pray from our heart. When I imagine this scriptural scene, I see how relationships, and community, can also help us. Jesus will work mercifully with us, wherever we are. Whether we are a Martha or a Mary, no matter our general personality, aptitude, or life-view, Jesus will be with us. And more, as Simon suggested as reasons for his delayed response, his love for us is so expansive that it embraces, and even surpasses, our stated desires.

Yet, a few questions linger. Will I remember to open my heart during future times of loss? Will I move beyond an intellectual exercise, rote prayers, and allow my entire being to open to God's magnificent graces? Will I allow myself to be surprised by God, to let God answer my prayers as God will?

Although written years prior to Simon's illness, it feels as though he was presciently writing to me about my own grief over his dying and death. Tom McMurray, SJ, reminds me that the risen Christ appeared through locked doors to his disheartened, fearful, and hidden disciples. Jesus hears my faint, tearful cries, through the walls of pain, shock, and denial. He will also break through any locked doors of fear, abandonment, and disbelief I create, or listen to from the evil spirit.

Belief in Jesus realigns my vision, and restores my heart and soul.

Questions to Consider: What are ways in which God counts on us to fulfill his mission on earth? How and when do we show our trust in Jesus? Apply this common saying to the practice of faith: "Seeing is believing." What has your experience been with grief? How has your faith interfaced with your grief? Jesus instructed people to remove Lazarus's burial clothing, and Simon suggested this as a precursor to our own shedding of our earthly bodies. Discuss this mystery in considering natural events, such as the acorn's shedding of its form into an oak tree.

The kingdom of God asks us to know that in times of crisis, in times of terrible personal loss, Jesus is asking us to wait, to trust that he will always act in love for us. By persistently turning to him and remembering his mission to the world, Jesus counts on disciples to help him to save the world from the fear of death.

14

Who or What Provides a Christian's True Security? (Luke 22:54–62)

A provocative analysis of why Peter—and by extension, other like-minded followers—have betrayed Jesus: At peak crisis, Peter was carrying a sword, and still reliant on the seductive but false promises of violence. Here we critically examine the reasons why people use violence. We also assert that when we do rely on violence in any form, rather than the word and power of God, we will fail, without having Jesus in our heart.

On Peter's Betrayal of Jesus

WHEN I REFLECT ON the story of the passion in Luke, I am struck by the theme of betrayal. Everyone betrays everyone else; everyone betrays himself. Pilate betrays his principles. So do the disciples. Every one of them fled from Jesus in his hour of need. Jesus is alone, the lone faithful figure in the narrative. This year, as every year, we hear about the betrayal of Peter. It's interesting that all four Gospels don't agree on much—even the words of the Eucharist are missing from John's Gospel. But all four Gospels agree: Peter betrayed Jesus. Peter told Jesus that he would always be faithful to him, then Jesus said, No, Peter. I don't think so. In fact, before the cock crows, you're going to deny three times that you even know me.

How did Jesus know that Peter would betray him? Jesus was divine and human. As God, I'm sure he knew the soul of Peter with divine insight.

But I believe that it was also obvious to Jesus as a human being that Peter was going to betray him. Why? Because Peter was still carrying a sword. I remember how, in the garden of Gethsemane, the garden of the great testing, Peter still carried a sword. Yes, he struck at the high priest's servant, cutting off his ear, I remember. After three years of living, eating, and drinking with Jesus, with him waking and sleeping, witnessing miracles and hearing him talk about faith in the Father and love of enemies—even watching Jesus heal the son of a centurion who was enforcing the military occupation of his land—Peter still carried a weapon. And I say, Jesus looked at that weapon, hanging there at Peter's side, and he said, "I don't think so." Jesus knew that Peter's promise of undying loyalty did not come from his trust of God; it sprang from his reliance on violence. He knew that Peter put faith in that sword, rather than in Jesus, and in the weapon, rather than in the Word of God.

Jesus knew. He knew that once Peter lost his sword, he would lose his bravery as well. Because Peter's courage resided in that weapon. Jesus listened to Peter's boastful promises of loyalty to the Prince of Peace, but as a perceptive man, saw clearly Peter's commitment to violence. When Jesus disarmed him—"Put your sword back into its sheath, for all who take the sword will perish by the sword"[1]—then Peter fled. Peter fled even while Jesus was being Jesus, not doing violence, but healing its effects—healing the terrible wound that Peter's violence had inflicted, healing the wound of a man who had come to arrest him—loving his enemy. It was as though Jesus was saying, "Peter, put away your weapon. Look! There is something greater, more powerful than violence here. It is my redeeming love. Put your faith in my healing power, not in the weapons of the kingdoms of this world. Peter, see this healing as a sign that the power of the Spirit of God, the power into whose hands I have committed my spirit, can overcome the violence of arms, will overcome even the violence of the cross."

But Peter was gone. Fled away. His hand, so wedded to weaponry, could not suddenly learn to heal. One so thoroughly weakened by the false vows of violence could not so soon embrace the valor of nonviolence.

Nor was his flight from Jesus ended with his escape from Gethsemane. He went on to betray him—I remember—once, twice, three times. So that in Gospel after Gospel after Gospel after Gospel, believers could see the so-called courage of the violent fully exposed. Weaponless, it is worthless.

---

1. Matt 26:52.

The sword serves only to shield a cowardice of the spirit. You cannot have a weapon in your hand, and Christ in your heart.

Something else. For years now—years—we in this country have been bleeding our courage into weapons. Hundreds of billions of dollars of weapons every year. Trillions in the last decades. And when, on September 11, 2001, it was shown that our weapons were of no avail, that despite the promises of the sword, the often-predicted specter of violence visited us, we too lost our courage. We too fled from Jesus, we too denied the Word of God: "Love your enemies, and pray for those who persecute you."[2] No! Not for us these words from the Word of God. They are as foreign to our hearts as was healing to the hand of Peter. We turned instead to more violence—the very thing that had deceived us. We declared war to be infinite—not God—and embarked on a journey of betrayal that has not ended to this day. Afghanistan. Iraq. Colombia. Haiti. Pakistan. Libya. Somalia. Yemen.

In the Scripture, we are told that after Peter's third betrayal Jesus turned and looked at Peter, and Peter, recalling Jesus' words, went out and wept bitterly. Would that we would do the same! Would that instead of cheering our violence, we would recall his words and weep bitterly at our betrayal!

But we are fleeing from him too fast to see his face, I fear.

Still, we are not without hope. Perhaps Jesus will yet be merciful to us and accost us on our way to do violence, as he interrupted the intended violence of Saul on the road to Damascus. "Saul! Saul! Why are you persecuting me?"[3] As disciples who want to be faithful to him in his passion, may we all pledge, at whatever cost to ourselves, to overcome evil with good, to oppose this rush to violence with our active nonviolence, to restrain the dogs of war and seek instead the face of Jesus. Before we who seek to live by the sword and finally die by the sword, let us pray in the words of the Psalm, "O Lord . . . restore us; if your face shine upon us, then we shall be safe."[4]

Philip's Reflection

Simon's lyrical and insightful reflection presents us with more indisputable proof of Jesus' direction to his followers to lay down our weapons, and rely

2. Matt 5:44.
3. Acts 9:4.
4. Ps 80:4.

upon the greater divine power of love, mercy, forgiveness, compassion, and healing. If we truly believed Jesus, we would do that. We may rationalize our refusal: Jesus was being idealistic and what he wants is impossible; it is easy for him because he is God; surely that does not apply to today's threats. Keeping with the theme of betrayal in this section of Christ's passion, let's examine the betrayal of violence. Then let's consider that Jesus' way—the power and love of God—guarantees that which violence pretends to, but can never fully provide.

My research and peace work indicate that people resort to violence for one or more of these reasons: to protect self or others' person or possessions; to fulfill a variety of self-interests, including the range of vicious desires; to exert or maintain control and/or domination over another or others, through threat or fear of harm; to demonstrate allegiance to local social demand or obligation, such as peremptory or retaliatory violence; or to respond to the nation-state call for violent punishment or intervention. The promises of violence are these: to add more days of life for self or others; to satisfy the urge to dominate another; to seek personal or apparent "justice" for a real or perceived crime through retaliation and punishment; to exert punishment for a crime to deter others; to elicit praise, gratitude, or glory; or to protect interests or status of those calling for and performing violence.

Violence is effective in accomplishing certain short-term goals—it may prolong our own or others' lives a bit longer, deter aggression, stop unwanted behavior, and provide social status. Peter used violence to try to protect Jesus, but he was lost when it failed. How did Peter feel when Jesus upbraided him, then healed the guard's ear? Peter represents humanity's understandable but futile reliance on violence in the face of danger—and its abject failure. The truth is that no amount of violence and killing in our personal or collective history has made us completely secure, or solved the timeless question, who or what survives this life? At the time of our death, all of the rationale and promises of violence dissolve.

Yet there are compelling cases to use violence. When I learned of governmental forces harming innocent people, such as the "disappearances" in many Central and South American countries, I felt, and feel, enraged. When I read of the courageous work by Jesuits and others in El Salvador through their adherence to the principles and practice of Liberation Theology, I was heartened. But when six of them were murdered by US-trained governmental agents in November, 1989, along with two other women seeking shelter,[5] I felt disgust and sadness. Surely those responsible, including their trainers, those ordering the murders, and especially those who killed deserved violent retribution. More broadly, are not violent revolutions against heinous governments justifiable? How might Jesus respond to these violently punitive or protective actions?

We sympathize with the oppressed, recognize their courage to act, even violently. God will judge those who use violence. Since Jesus does not condone violence, *and* wants us to creatively work with the oppressed for liberation and a more just world, followers must again turn to Jesus' ways.[6] We recall that God decided to embody God's Word amidst an oppressive, violent empire, choosing *not* to become a king or general, presumably employing the violence constitutive to those positions. Immediately after his baptism, Jesus *was* tempted by Satan to accomplish his salvific mission in just that way: by using Satan's means of violence, terror, fear, chaos, and domination. But Jesus refused those methods, preached creative, active resistance to oppression, and remained faithful to the Father of mercy, forgiveness, compassion, and love.

I can think of no more valid justification for violence in humanity's history than its use to protect Jesus' life. But Jesus is teaching us that a God-force is required to overcome evil, and to provide our ultimate security. Incidentally, that powerful force is purposely obscured and demeaned by those who rely on the seductive but false promises of violence.

Through Jesus, God reveals practical answers to our problems of evil and death. We are to resist evil in creative, nonviolent ways that restore dignity to the oppressed, and offer a return to humanity, and the kingdom, to the lost oppressors. Our "weapons" are returning good for evil, forgiving endlessly, praying for our persecutors, and loving all others in an agapeistic way. Such actions require great courage and reliance on God.

We are called to put our faith in the power that Jesus embodied: the power of his promise of eternal life. That promise cannot be fulfilled through violence. As with any aspect of discipleship, I need to continually call on God's love and grace to help me remain on the path of true salvation.

Questions to Consider: Explore and discuss the fact that even after living with Jesus for three years, Peter was still carrying and using a weapon. As God, Jesus is omniscient. What is your reaction to the proposition that

5. See Brackley, "Remembering the Jesuit," for information.
6. See Wink, *Jesus and Nonviolence*, 5–6.

Jesus knew Peter would betray him because he was carrying a weapon? Applying a lesson learned from Peter's betrayal and abandonment of Jesus, discuss this statement: Courage in the face of physical harm resides in the possession and use of powerful self-defense ability and/or overwhelming weaponry. Discuss this statement: Surely violence, though insufficiently used, was justified to protect Jesus.

The kingdom of God requires us to have the faith and courage—or to pray for deepening of faith and courage—to know that our true security and ultimate survival is assuredly in God's hands, not the hearts and hands that carry weapons.

15

Jesus' Nonviolent Conversion of Death: Running with Open Hearts to His Empty Tomb (John 20:1-18)

Simon proposes an inspired way of understanding Jesus' sacrificial death and salvific resurrection: God's essential nature of nonviolent, healing love is manifested in Jesus' nonviolent conversion of death from enemy to ally. We can acknowledge his resurrection intellectually, but as the Beloved Disciple shows us, when we enter Jesus' empty tomb with the mystery of divine love, we will be gifted the faith to believe, even without rational understanding.

The Resurrection

TODAY, WE RUN IN our imaginations to see the empty tomb where Jesus had lain in death. We can run with Peter, the head of the church. But if we run with the Beloved Disciple, if we run with love, we will arrive ahead of the head. If we arrive with the head, we may be the first to cross the threshold. But if we enter the mystery with love, we will be the first to find faith: to believe in his resurrection even without yet understanding.

I have a personal story about my ongoing journey to understand what the resurrection of Jesus means—and why so many don't believe in it.

We will be told soon in this Gospel that we are blessed if we believe without seeing. In some cases, like the real presence in the bread and wine, we are to believe despite what we see. But truly, in hearing that Jesus "conquered death," my belief is strained. In one of our eucharistic acclamations, we say or sing, "Dying you destroyed our death . . ."[1] Death destroyed, done away with, eliminated. Can anyone believe that?

I can't. Death has been too real for me—in my personal life, and in my ministry. In my own life, as in the lives of many, death has taken my grandparents and parents. Death has taken my teachers and my students, my friends, and my Jesuit brothers. I remember speaking with a Jesuit brother of mine from New England, who returned home to bury his father. He told me he was going alone to the undertaker because his mother was in the hospital with pneumonia, and his only sibling was dead.

In my ministry, I have traveled to places like Iraq, where UN sanctions and US weapons have inflicted death on a scale that still overwhelms my imagination. And what can we say of the genocide in Rwanda or in Darfur? What shall we "believers" say to friends and family who remain? How can we, with any rationality—with any compassion at all—say to those who mourn that Jesus has destroyed death?

The answer for me came from a different direction—from my belief in the nonviolence of Jesus. Jesus eloquently preached and powerfully practiced love of enemies during his life and I believe he also practiced it in his encounter with death. Nonviolence does not seek to defeat, destroy, or do away with the enemy. Active nonviolence seeks to engage the enemy so as to convert him or her from unjust and violent ways. Nonviolence enters into dialogue, into communion, and, one might even venture to say, into community with the enemy. Nonviolence seeks to eliminate the enemy by transforming the enemy into a friend. And yes, in loving one's enemy, one is also transformed.

This is the path that Jesus pursued in his engagement with death: the path of nonviolence. That is why death is still around. Jesus didn't do away with death. Our divine satyagrahi (Gandhi's word for a nonviolent warrior) entered into communion with death until he converted it.

It makes sense to me, the conversion of the enemy, death. It makes sense because it fits with the way Jesus taught and lived—especially with his enemies. It makes sense because it took Jesus three days to accomplish this conversion. The destruction that is characteristic of violence, on the other hand, is instant. One "bang" from a gun and it's over. It doesn't take much love—in fact, one must "turn off" one's love to do it. But the

---

1. "Acclamations in the Eucharistic Prayer," 2.

healing of nonviolence—like all healing—takes longer. The healing love of nonviolence is born out of profound respect for the other. The love of the nonviolent person must be deep and unfathomable, even to the depths of hell—which is where Jesus went to preach to the dead.

It makes sense to me because death, which before this day had separated us from God, now leads us to God. We were taught as children that Jesus "opened the gates of heaven"—and there's something to that. In all those Greek and Roman and Babylonian myths, the gods were immortal, we were mortal. Hence, death drew an uncrossable dividing line between humans doomed to die and gods who would never and could never feel death's threat or its pangs. But Jesus has with Easter Day converted death. In fact, death has become his disciple, uniting us with "[his] Father and [our] Father, with [his] God and [our] God."[2]

The true depth of God's nonviolent love is revealed on Easter because when Jesus entered transformative communion with death, he allowed death to change him, too. As the church fathers wrote, "Without him we were unable to live; without us, he was unable to die." The change that Jesus underwent in his engagement with death is this: when the Father brings Jesus back into his bosom, the Father receives mortality into the Trinity. So it is that we mortals who follow Jesus now have in him not only our path into heaven, but our way into the very heart of God. Into such mysteries, angels—because they are immortal—cannot peer.

So that we might now begin to live that new, nonviolent life, Jesus sends us his Holy Spirit—the very same Spirit by which he lived and through whose power he rose from the dead. Each time that I see death in my life or in my mission, I have to make an act of faith in this Spirit, in the resurrection of Jesus. Just as with the Eucharist, I seek to go beyond what my eyes observe, and to see with the eyes of faith: that these mortals so beloved are even now being gathered up to God. And that we who mourn them will be comforted by that same Spirit.

And even more: The death that Jesus was raised from was the death of oppression. The state and religious powers exercised their supreme authority over Jesus until they oppressed him to death. And when the Spirit raised Jesus, it was that death that the Spirit raised him from—from the death of oppression. If I live by that Spirit, God will grant me an inexhaustible source for resisting oppression, and moving with Jesus toward reconciliation and life. That's hard for me, because I'm always tempted to challenge oppression

2. John 20:17.

out of (self-) "righteous anger." But that is, in my heart, a defection to the kingdoms of this world.

But think of what could have happened if we had brought this belief in the resurrection to the events of September 11, 2001. Would we have sworn allegiance to the very violence we said we abhorred? Would we out of fear have enslaved our economy to the production of weapons? Would we have declared war to be everlasting—instead of the mercy of God? No. In our love we would have found ways to pursue our enemies even to the depths of hell—until we transformed them into disciples of the king of justice and mercy, and our whole world into the resurrection community of love.

I want to have the courage to love my enemies as Jesus commanded and empowered me to do. I believe God the Holy Trinity will give me this courage because God sent his son Jesus to "free those who, through fear of death had become subject to slavery all their life."[3]

I want to live this nonviolent life—his life—because I believe in the resurrection from oppression and life everlasting. Amen.

Philip's Reflection

Who can effectively think through irrationalities like death, and evil? Our minds alone are insufficient to grasp those mysterious realities. Though a committed Christian, I struggle with the shattering power of death. Simon made an important distinction between our mind and heart when attempting to grasp the resurrection, and proposed something I never considered.

The first important reminder is for me to pray at the empty tomb with my heart opened, like Saint John. I analyze life. That was useful when I studied and applied psychology, when I taught literature, and when I analyzed social systems. But probably like all personal strengths, my analytical ability has its drawbacks. If I rely solely on my analytical powers to understand mysteries like suffering and death allowed by an all-loving God, my inability to satisfactorily understand can lead to despair. I expect that if I could fully understand, I could better accept. Instead, I have learned that acceptance precedes, and often helps increase, my limited understanding.

Hope stirs when I prayerfully contemplate Simon's unique insight about death-as-convert. When we follow Jesus, even into the enormous struggles against humanity's deep hatred, destructiveness, and oppression—and for too many, death caused by those evils—Jesus ultimately leads

3. Heb 2:15.

us into his nonviolent conversion of death and straight into the embrace of the Trinity.

The notion of death being a vehicle to heaven is not new. In John Donne's Holy Sonnet 6, the speaker derides death, then concludes that after serving its larger purpose of transport to God, death will die. But my brother's insight is magnificent: Jesus employed the means of the infinitely loving nonviolent God to "win death over" to the service of the good. Naturally, Jesus would be consistent with his ministry even after death, and prior to his resurrection. If death can now truly be considered a converted friend, that certainly adds a nuanced and vital layer of meaning to Paul's assertion that "all things work for the good for those who love God . . ."[4]

Although the head is a part of our grappling with mysteries, if we first open our hearts, we can indeed more fully grasp the undying love of the resurrected Jesus.

Questions to Consider: Although Christ's resurrection is central to Christianity, have you ever had difficulty in believing that he "destroyed death"? Why did Jesus take three days to rise? Recall an experience with dying or death that has meaning for you. Where has Jesus been with you around that memorable experience? Which biblical character in this scriptural reading do you most identify with, and why? How does the resurrection help us cope with death—others' and our own?

The path to the kingdom of God has been paved by Jesus' nonviolent conversion of death from an enemy who separates us, to a friend who delivers us home for a joyful reunion.

4. Rom 8:28.

16

How Should Christian Communities Treat Internal Dissenters? (John 20:24–30)

Using the model of the apostles' patience with the disbelieving Thomas, we can emulate how a Christian community "suffers the presence" of one of their own who refuses to accept a critical faith component. We recognize the influence of surrounding culture on our impatience. Our desire for uniformity and "purity" of beliefs is understandable. But because empires, such as the one the early apostles lived under, seek to divide and dominate, divisiveness among the subjugated actually serves to perpetuate those kingdoms. When the other apostles kept Thomas within their community, they acted in an anti-imperial way, in harmony with the liberatory kingdom of God. Until we truly rely on the power of the Spirit to author our daily faith, we succumb to the divisions common today, and thereby miss a key, differentiating, and edifying element of God's kingdom: patient and steadfast witness—just as Jesus acts with each of us.

Thomas the Unbeliever

TODAY WE HEAR A familiar story, the story of "Doubting Thomas." I want to go back to the story again and put it in context and, if I can, see what was happening and what was at stake in this narrative of Thomas, the apostles, and our Lord Jesus.

A generation or so before Jesus was born, there had been a great struggle between two superpowers for control of the Western world—Greece and Rome. About thirty years before Jesus was born, Rome won a decisive battle, and then there was only one empire. One sole remaining superpower in the world. This sole remaining superpower brought its massive military superiority to the Middle East and conquered the small Middle Eastern nation of Israel. They conquered it easily; but they had a lot of trouble holding onto it. The people in that Middle Eastern country simply didn't want to be ruled by the empire.

I studied Latin for four years in high school. When I went to college, I majored in Latin and Greek. In all those years, all I heard about was "the glory that was Greece, and the grandeur that was Rome." The Roman Empire certainly had a lot to say for itself. There were the Roman roads and sewage systems. There was Roman law and urban culture. They provided a worldwide economy with a universal currency—imagine! And a universal language: everyone could either speak or write Latin. Yes, the Romans had a lot going for themselves—and there was a big payoff for being part of their empire.

But in those eight years of Jesuit, Catholic education, no one ever asked the question, "What if you didn't want to be part of the empire?" You know, "Thanks a lot for the sewers and the money, but no."

One way to see the Gospels is as stories of a fiercely proud people who simply didn't want to be ruled by the empire. They resisted in all kinds of ways—from the temple worship of the Sadducees to the "people piety" of the Pharisees to the apocalypticism of Qumranians. From the open, armed rebellion of the Zealots to the shadowy assassinations of fanatic individuals the Romans called "sicarii."

In the end, all those groups actually served the empire, because the empire's way of domination was "divida et impera": "divide and dominate." Set the groups off against each other, and they'll be so busy fighting they will never unite to overthrow the empire. Get them arguing about what kinds of vessels to use in the temple, get them to ostracize one another over sexual behavior, banish one another over political beliefs, or excommunicate one another over differences in faith. Divide, separate them from each other: "divida et impera." Divide and dominate.

This is the world into which our Lord Jesus came. And we know how he acted. Understanding that world, we can perhaps now understand the impossible, revolutionary power of his words when he said, "I will not reject anyone who comes to me."[1] So different from the empire, yes, from the "kingdoms of this world," from the constant dividing of "us" from "them." Our Lord will never turn anyone away who comes to him.

Maybe the world in which Jesus lived sounds familiar to us. Too familiar. Maybe more so if we know people from Iraq, Afghanistan, or Palestine today. I remember when I was a kid, I read that Jesus had fed five thousand men—not counting women and children (which is still a problem in the Catholic Church: the discounting of women)—five thousand men at one sitting. I didn't disbelieve the miracle. I figured Jesus could multiply loaves and fishes, what's the problem? What I had trouble believing was that five thousand guys would be following Jesus around, as one Gospel says, for three days. Coming from a working-class family, I couldn't believe that. Five thousand people? Three whole days? Why weren't they at *work*? It served the empire then, and the empire now, to have the people hungry and scrambling for work. That way they never could rebel against their overlords.

But Jesus feeds the people, and, more than that, forms them into a new community. He had them sit down in groups of "fifty." It turns out that the Greek word for "fifty" is "Pentecost." "Have the people sit down in groups of [Pentecost],"[2] said Jesus. Then he took the bread, blessed it, broke it, and gave it to the disciples, who gave it to the people. And afterward, there were as many baskets left over as there were tribes of Israel.

I remember how the gospel tells us that Jesus healed whole villages of people who were sick. I didn't believe that one, either. Oh, I believed in the healing part, just not that everyone in the village could be sick.

Then I went to Iraq.[3] UNICEF did a study of the effects of the sanctions on Iraq after the first eight years. They compared the death rate for Iraqi children under the age of five before and after the sanctions. UNICEF determined that the sanctions had increased the number of deaths among Iraqi children under the age of five by five hundred thousand. Five hundred thousand children under the age of five, dead because of the US/UN sanctions. And that was just toddlers. UNICEF didn't count the other ages of

---

1. John 6:37.

2. Luke 9:14.

3. Simon, with members of Voices in the Wilderness, made several trips there during the sanctions. After returning, he did numerous presentations about the devastating, lethal human cost to the Iraqis.

people.[4] So . . . a whole village of sick people? Yes. When I went to Iraq I saw—I saw and believed.

And what about all those possessed people Jesus kept healing? Can we find any parallel today? Well, suppose someone had been tortured at Abu Ghraib, Camp Bucca, Guantanamo, or any of the other secret camps the CIA runs. Suppose even worse, that one of their family members was tortured or killed. Suppose their daughters and wives were raped and the soldiers exonerated. Suppose your house were blown up and your whole family killed. What would happen? Wouldn't you be seized by hate, possessed by rage and a lust to avenge yourself? You'd go mad with that desire. You wouldn't care about anything else. You'd be possessed. But wait— haven't I just described a suicide bomber?

I remember when Jesus was casting out the demon from the Gadarene man, and Jesus asked his name. What did the possessor say? "My name is Legion."[5] I'm sure the people of that Middle Eastern country understood that name. The man was possessed by a legion. The land was possessed . . . Jesus was doing all this because he wanted the people to revolt in a different way. To love their enemies.

Now we are drawing very close to our story today. The Romans had a way of handling people who acted against the empire, who fed and ate with people whom the rulers had said to cast out, who healed the people whom the empire wanted wounded, who united in thanksgiving the people that the empire wanted to divide into recriminations. They crucified them.

You could be crucified for only one crime in the Roman Empire, but first you had to be a noncitizen—no Roman citizen could be crucified, it was too terrible a way to die. The cross was reserved for noncitizens convicted in a Roman court of being an insurgent against the empire. That's the crime—insurgency against the empire—that Jesus was crucified for.

---

4. See Geneva International Centre for Justice, "Razing the Truth." This comprehensive article contains the UNICEF figures Simon cited, and includes subsequent attempts by some to debunk the numbers of child deaths from the sanctions. Destroying their infrastructure and maintaining a blockade was a US-planned military strategy. For the Christian, entering an argument over the accurate number of deaths caused directly by the blockade and sanction implies acceptance and legitimacy of the action. Engaging in a debate on the actual death toll forces this morally impossible question: How many children and people killed are acceptable? Ancient empires once used our government's tactic, called "siege warfare." The military premise was that the resulting starvation and civilian deaths—the intended outcome—would force the enemy to overthrow their leader, or that he would abdicate because of the carnage and death.

5. Luke 8:30.

That's what he says to us, what it takes for us to become his disciples: to "take up that cross every day, and follow [him].[6] And God forbid, Paul says, "But may I never boast except in the cross of our Lord Jesus Christ."[7]

But wait, the story is not ended. The empire did all that it could do to silence this man who had embraced all. Then God did what only God could do. God raised Jesus from the dead. God overcame what was the ultimate controlling power of the empire, "setting free those who, through fear of death had become subject to slavery all their life."[8]

Thomas would not believe it. Could not believe it. How could he? It was ridiculous not to believe in the power of death, and in the power of those who could inflict death. Insane.

And note: we say "doubting Thomas," but doubting is not what Thomas was doing. Doubting is saying "Well, maybe yes, maybe no. I don't know. I'm not sure." But Thomas was saying, in effect, "You guys are all deluded for believing that Jesus rose from the dead. No way. I'm not going to buy into this! I'll have to put my finger into the holes in his hands and my hand into his side before I'm going to believe it."[9]

And one more look. This thing that Thomas was denying, that he was refusing to believe was not some tenet of lesser importance in our faith. It was the central teaching of our faith. "For if Christ has not been raised," says Paul, "[our] faith is [in] vain."[10] The real Thomas was not doubting Thomas but disbelieving Thomas. Whatever else you might say about the doctrines of our faith, the resurrection is absolutely crucial. If you don't believe Jesus has been raised from the dead, then really you don't believe in Jesus our Savior.

Can anyone imagine such a person being included in a Christian community? Should he or she not be excommunicated, banished, shunned, or at least avoided? Sadly, many in our church would think so. Well, the apostles didn't. Somehow, they found a way to keep Thomas around. "Now a week later, his disciples were again inside and Thomas was with them."[11] Thomas, the one who refused to believe the thing that made Christians Christian? That Thomas? The one sitting there with his arms crossed saying, "I don't think so"? What kind of community must they have been to

6. Luke 9:23.
7. Gal 6:14.
8. Heb 2:15.
9. See John 20:25.
10. 1 Cor 15:17.
11. John 20:26.

stay in communion with such a man as Thomas, who could not accept our teaching?

I think this: they were a community that had already begun to distinguish itself from the divisions the empire so ardently desired. By suffering the presence of Thomas, they began the revolution against violence and domination that was characteristic of the empire, and began turning toward the inclusivity that was characteristic of Jesus. By holding Thomas in community, they began to live out their belief that the resurrection was stronger than the strength of the empire. They knew that if they kept Thomas and kept praying, then one day Jesus—who is the author of all our faith—would come to Thomas, in Jesus' own time, and suiting Thomas' own way.

The name Thomas means "twin" in Aramaic. And so I have to ask: does Thomas have twins here in this era, in our faith community? Are there twins of Thomas today whom the law and the dividers tell us we must exclude from the community of faith? And when we identify them, or they identify themselves to us, shall we act then in conformity to the empire or according to the transformation of our minds in Christ? Will we let our adherence to the law banish the Thomases of our time? Or will we embrace them with the love of Jesus, praying with perfect patience, yes, perhaps even suffering their presence, until Jesus comes to them in his own time, and in their own way?

One final thought—a poem, really—from another Thomas who lived about twelve centuries after the Thomas in the Gospels. He was a bit of a rebel himself—an intellectual one. In fact, he got himself in trouble with some pious Catholics, and some of them burned the books he wrote. Maybe you know him by his full name, Thomas d'Aquino or Thomas Aquinas. This is what he wrote one day, speaking from the perspective of Jesus:

> Because of my compassion, the sun wanted to be near me all night
> And the earth deeded her fields to me,
> And all in heaven said,
> "We have voted you our governor; tell us your divine mandate."
> And I did, and God will never revoke it:
> Nothing in existence is ever turned away.
> More tender is my Lord's heart than any heart has ever been.
> So, when the divine realm asked me to govern it with one simple rule,
> I looked into His eyes and then knew what to say to any angel who might
>   serve as a sentry to God:
> No creature should ever be turned away.[12]

12. Ladinsky, ed., *Love Poems*, 127–28. See Harak, ed., *Aquinas and Empowerment*, for further reading on Aquinas.

It was a week later and the apostles were gathered. And Thomas—Thomas was with them!

Philip's Reflection

Using one *disbelieving* apostle and his community's response, Simon considered three distinct but interconnected aspects of the kingdom of God. Early apostles faced forces opposing the realization of God's kingdom. First, the ambient culture—especially a dominative one like an occupying empire—held an extremely powerful influence in shaping what inhabitants believed and determined as normative or even possible. Next, individuals immersed in life's twin realities of evil and death, both intensified under military occupation, were skeptical of full deliverance from either or both. Third, societal constructs promoted uniformity, and often ostracized and excluded dissenters.

Those opposing forces remain particularly strong and vocal today. But the early Christian community offered specific ways in countering them. We are to suffer our own malcontents; continue to provide membership and share with them our experience of God; pray on their behalf; encourage them to continue to pray; and expect Jesus to reach them in his time and individualized ways.

Jesus taught and provided modeling of how to act as God desires within the imperial world of dominative power, and the continual threat of violence and execution. To enact the Lord's Prayer, like him, we must continually act with unlimited mercy and forgiveness; love everyone, even in the face of evil; resist the empire's (or any nation-state's) alluring call to violence—for whatever stated rationale, like "freedom" or "protecting our way of life"—and put no ideology or person above Jesus.

Life's painful realities provide fertile ground for our misgivings about the miracle of the resurrection. But at the end of John's reading, Jesus calls *us* blessed—we who believe and have not seen him in person. We are blessed with freely given faith from God. It becomes easier for me to be compassionate with myself, as God is with me, when I recall that at times his disciples struggled with disbelief and fear.

The last element that Simon emphasized recounts the faithfulness and patience of the community when "dealing with" Thomas. Their patience with him mirrored Jesus' patience, and was inspired by the Holy Spirit. Our way of living should fit into Jesus' ways. As Gandhi said once, "There is just the same inviolable connection between the means and the end as there is between the seed and the tree."[13] An essential component of Christianity is to follow *the ways* that Jesus taught us to live: continually, patiently loving all others as he and Thomas's friends did, even though we may not live to see the tree.

Questions to Consider: Jesus lived under the occupation of the Roman Empire. He taught a nonviolent liberation from their particular—and all peoples'—oppression. Identify as many specific ways in which he taught resistance to oppression. Identify similarities between the Roman Empire and the United States. How did those disciples who saw the resurrected Jesus treat Thomas? How does that early Christian community provide specific ways in which we should treat others today? Where does the quality of patience fit within your own faith journey, and within God's kingdom?

Those dwelling in the kingdom of God mirror the Trinity's love, patience, welcoming, unifying, and steadfast witness.

13. Bombay Sarvodaya Mandal and Gandhi Research Foundation, "Means and Ends."

17

We Enact God-Like Love When We Forgive
Enemies and Friends (John 21:1–20)

Although forgiving enemies is difficult, forgiving betrayal by loved ones
can be even harder. Here we discuss the specific ways in which Jesus
forgave both his persecutors and his close friend Peter. When we begin
to grasp with mind and heart the magnitude of the power of God's
loving forgiveness, we are moved to make that a primary action in all
our relationships.

Forgiving Peter

ONE OF THE BEST things about Jesus is that he not only tells us that we have
to forgive others, and love our enemies, he shows us how in his own life. I
love that, because it means that our nonviolence is not based so much on
principles or practicality—though to live nonviolently is the most practical
of principles. It means that our nonviolent life is the natural expression
of our relationship with Jesus; it emerges from and returns to the love we
share with him. Or, put another way: Jesus gives us the Holy Spirit so that
we can love and forgive as he did. I remember how "he breathed upon them
and said to them, 'Receive the Holy Spirit. Whose sins you forgive are forgiven them . . .'"[1]

As it says in the Canon of the Mass, "He sent the Holy Spirit from you,
Father, as his first gift to those who believe, to complete his work on earth,

---

1. John 20:22–23.

and to bring us to the fullness of grace."[2] So I'm remembering what Jesus has done with the power of the Spirit, so that we his beloved can anticipate what we can also do with his Spirit.

We see Jesus' forgiveness and love of enemies all through his life, but especially when it is most difficult—during his passion and death. Do you remember how he forbade his disciples to protect him when the religious authorities came to arrest him? Jesus knew they were going to take him to his death, but he still told his disciples, "Put your sword back into its sheath, for all who take the sword will perish by the sword."[3] Because the apostles still didn't understand, and one of them, we think Peter, had used his sword to cut off the ear of the servant of the high priest. Jesus not only rebuked Peter, he healed the ear of one of the high priest's servants. The one who was arresting him—who was taking him to his death. He healed him! Love your enemies.

Just the other day, I received an email from one of my friends, trying to justify our attacks and occupation of Iraq as "defending Christendom."[4] Even if this rather strange assertion were true, the gospel story of Jesus' arrest would make us wonder. If the Word of God forbade the use of violence to defend Christ himself, how can we justify violence to defend "Christendom"?

But of course, Jesus' forgiving of his enemies doesn't stop there. He also forgives them from the cross—not from the glory of the resurrection, but from the cross! In the midst of all that mortal pain, in the midst of his sorrow unto death, and in the midst of his unrepentant and even scornful crucifiers, Jesus forgave his enemies, praying for his persecutors: "Father forgive them, they know not what they do."[5]

But you know, it's one thing to forgive your enemies—you expect them to try to do evil to you. But what about your loved ones? What if a person you love, a person you've put faith in, a person you've entrusted your deepest heart to—what happens if your dear friend betrays you? How do you forgive such a thing? How do you love again, trust again, find your

2. Just, ed., "Basic Texts."

3. Matt 26:52.

4. See International Committee of the Red Cross, for delineation of Geneva Convention. Directly targeting noncombatants in war, as well as collective punishment, violates the Geneva Convention. Incidentally, those actions also violate a condition of JWT. Simon wrote this reflection in 2003, around the time of our second, prolonged and devastating bombing attack on the defenseless Iraqi civilian population.

5. Luke 23:34.

way back to friendship again? No rules here, no principles. As always, we look to Jesus. Let's watch Jesus and his friend Peter.

We all know the story. After boldly claiming that he would never betray Jesus, that he would stay faithful to his friend even if everyone else failed, later that very same evening, Peter betrayed Jesus. Not once, not twice, but three times. Three betrayals. Three denials. Three violations of their trust. " [A]nd the Lord turned and looked at Peter [,] . . . and [Peter] went out and began to weep bitterly."[6]

Now I believe that when Jesus uttered that astonishing prayer of forgiveness from the cross—from the cross!—he forgave Peter, too. He forgave all of us. But you know: He wants to speak to each of us personally about his forgiveness for us. He's not only the savior of the world, he's my personal savior. The savior of each one of us. So, the Jesus I know is going to go looking for Peter. And he's not going to stop until Peter knows, personally, that Jesus has forgiven him.

And something more, I think. Jesus wants not just to forgive Peter, but to restore their lost trust, their lost relationship. And if I know Jesus, he's going to want not just to restore the relationship, but to make it better than before. Deeper, more solid, more loving than before the betrayal. Something that Peter will want to tell the whole world about.

How is Jesus going to accomplish that? Let's see.

I notice how Jesus doesn't go to the sensitive part right away. He starts slowly to reestablish the relationship. First, he helps them in their fishing work. Then he gives a sign of how generous the restoration will be: they've never caught so many fish.

Then the next step. Jesus prepares a meal for all of them—letting Peter know he is still part of Jesus' community, under his care, an object of his attention, someone Jesus still wants to share table fellowship with. Surely Peter must feel more at ease now, though still apprehensive, I should think.

Suppose you had betrayed a friend, as Peter had. If you could ever even work up the courage to approach your friend again, if you could ever overcome your shame enough to talk to him, what would you say? "Can you ever, ever forgive me? And . . . do you still love me? Can you ever be my friend again?"

But before Peter gets a chance to ask Jesus, instead Jesus asks Peter, "Simon, son of John, do you love me?"[7] What is Jesus doing here? He's being

6. Luke 22:61–62.
7. John 21:15.

98

Jesus. Taking the sins of the world, taking the sins of Peter, upon himself. It's as though he is saying to Peter,

> Peter, I know that you could have lived your whole life thinking you were a stand-up guy. But then I came into your life, and now you can't think that about yourself any more. And now that I've done that to you, I want to know, "Do you still love me?" And Peter, you probably could have gone through your whole life thinking you were the kind of guy who'd never abandon his friends. And then I came into your life, and now you can't think that about yourself anymore. And I want to know, after I've done that to you, do you want to be my friend?

How wonderful a friend is Jesus! Good, good friends will find a way to find fault with themselves when there's a problem in the relationship. They'll find a way to share the guilt with you somehow. For the sake of staying in relationship, they don't want to leave you alone in your apology—even if you're the one at fault. The same with Jesus. So here he is, finding a way of apologizing for being God.

Now I can see two things we can learn about Jesus from his reconciliation with Peter. The first is that Jesus really appreciates how difficult it is to be his disciple, and to be his friend. We see that here, and earlier too, at the Last Supper, when he washed his disciples' feet. When we fail, Jesus understands. To even the most bitter betrayal, he responds with love, forgiveness, and—amazingly—with an invitation to an even more intimate relationship with him in the Spirit.

And the second is this. Imagine if you had committed some sin. Any sin, no matter how terrible. And you came to Peter and said, "Peter, do you know what I did?" Peter would say, "No, you know what *I* did?" I believe that now, Jesus wanted Peter to be the head of his church, because he wanted forgiveness to be the head of his church. Remembering this profound betrayal, and this even more profound reconciliation, there would be no sin that Peter would not forgive.

And so it must be with us, his disciples. As strong a stand as we might take, as we must take, on the moral issues of our time, as powerfully we might speak out against the killing in war, in abortion, in the death penalty, we must speak even more about the grace of forgiveness for these sins. We must first be a home that welcomes and loves sinners.

Philip's Reflection

Simon highlights essential components of Jesus' reconciling and subsequent strengthening of Peter's fractured relationship with him. Through Jesus' wondrous interaction, we learn how to act lovingly, compassionately, and forgivingly.

Jesus' forgiveness of Peter had a profound influence on Simon. He was deeply touched by Jesus' acts of friendship and reparation of the damage to Peter by his renunciations. Good friends—animated by the Spirit—will not allow another friend to take all the blame on themselves. I warmly recall that Simon and I practiced that in our relationship.

How merciful and compassionate of Jesus to consider the cost of discipleship on *us*. At the time of Peter's denial, clearly his faith was still developing. Several years after his reconciliation, he would passionately preach and live the gospel, and courageously die a martyr. How do I foster the desire to become more holy, forgiving, compassionate, loving, and courageous, and like Peter, to offer my earthly life in witness and service to Jesus?

As I began my second layperson's Ignatian retreat, my director, Tom McMurray, SJ, asked me to describe Jesus' face as Jesus gazed upon me. I invite the reader to do the same. There was a lot of filtering I had to account for, and then put aside. Was it really Jesus who was looking at me, or some projection of mine? The Creator has loved me and us into existence, and Jesus and the Spirit sustain and guide us in our journey towards liberation and homecoming. Prayerfully returning to Jesus' healing interaction with Peter deepens my awareness that God forgives me. That grace helps me to see myself through Jesus' eyes, and to practice unrestricted, unlimited forgiveness of myself and others. Since forgiveness is a hallmark of the church, it needs to be an essential component in my journey with Jesus.

I have always been fond of Peter. I selected his as my confirmation name fifty years ago. His words and actions make him real to me: a conscientious married man who appears impulsive. I recall his sinking while walking miraculously on the water towards Jesus, his affirming answer that Jesus was indeed "the Messiah, the Son of the living God."[8] And of course, his triple renunciation. Peter was a passionate and flawed believer. Like me.

We are fortunate to have a God who showed through his actions how to live his words. And he gave us the Holy Spirit so that we can accomplish the harder parts, like forgiving self, enemies, and those closest. In prayer,

8. Matt 16:16.

God brings me to places in need of reconciliation. Sometimes I am challenged to forgive other Christians who speak or act in ways I think are antithetical to Christ's words and actions. Before I forgive, I acknowledge to myself and to God my true feelings. I invite Jesus and the Spirit to stand with me, and I listen. God reminds me to be humble and to remember that the person or people with whom I am in conflict are God's children too, as dear to God as I. God gently reminds me of times God graciously and lovingly forgave me. I call on that same grace-filled source to help me forgive, however imperfectly, partly to thank and honor God for his love and forgiveness. I often need to repeat that process until forgiveness takes deeper hold in my heart.

During those grace-filled times of forgiveness, I am both participating in and helping build the kingdom of God. Then it is easier to hold the gazes of my brother, Peter, the saints, and Jesus himself, smiling at me.

Questions to Consider: Delineate and discuss the ways Jesus shows us how to forgive others. Reflect upon, then write or discuss this observation: Jesus gives us the Holy Spirit so that we can love and forgive as he did. Reflect upon Jesus' forgiveness of his friend and disciple, Peter. From that interaction, what can we apply to our close relationships and faith community? Does our forgiveness by Jesus and our forgiveness of others have any impact in our beliefs and actions concerning important issues like abortion, capital punishment, clergy child abuse, war, pandemic behavior, and others? Recall the elements of a memorable reconciliation. What made it memorable, effective, or ineffective?

Those who dwell in the kingdom of God rely on the Holy Spirit to forgive all sins committed by self and others—as Jesus, the Word of God, has done and continues to do.

18

We Are One with Christ Jesus

These final two chapters examine the inspirational lives of two martyred disciples of Christ. Here we apply Saint Cecilia's witness, courage, and martyrdom as a means of more completely understanding how Jesus wants us to live with each other. Unlike earthly nations—like her Roman one and ours today—with societal stratifications, and privileged and oppressed peoples, in the kingdom of God, we are all equally valued. Therefore, it is against our faith and our religion to dehumanize by condemning anyone's personal or social identities, by fostering or supporting racism, sexism, or any other discrimination.

St. Cecilia

YEARS AFTER THE DEATH of Saint Cecilia, she became known as the patroness of music—the patroness of song. I have two pieces of information about Saint Cecilia that changed my view of her. I'll start with the "patroness of music" part.

It appears that Saint Cecilia became the patron saint of music not because of anything she did. It appears she became the patron saint of music through a scribal error. After the fall of the Roman Empire, people lost the knowledge of how to speak Latin, even though a lot of ancient documents—especially the documents of the church—were written in Latin. So, monks in the monasteries over the years preserved the heritage of Western civilization by laboriously hand-copying the ancient documents. Some of them knew Latin, and some didn't. But we have many of our ancient records because of the endless devotion of those monks. Still, as one might imagine, over the years some errors were bound to creep in.

One of those errors occurred in writing the story of Saint Cecilia. It seems that Cecilia was fleeing her father, and possibly the man whom her father had arranged for her to marry. When she found refuge in one of the baths that the Romans and Greeks were so fond of, her father ordered that the heat and the steam in the bath be turned up to maximum, in an attempt to drive her back out. But Cecilia didn't come out. She refused to come out. Cecilia stayed there in that bath, stayed there stubbornly resisting the will of her father and official fiancé, stayed until she suffocated to death in the steam and the heat.

The way this is written in Latin is *mortuit pipis calientibus*, "She died with the (steam) pipes being red-hot." But over the years of copying, the *l* and the *i* of *calientibus* got merged somehow, and it came out *pipis canentibus*—not "with the pipes being red-hot," but "with the pipes *singing*." So that's how Cecilia became the patron saint of music. Looks like a mistake, huh? Sometimes she's actually depicted as playing an organ—with the pipes singing, even though organs weren't invented until way after Cecilia's lifetime. Cecilia, music, singing—all a mistake?

Maybe not, I'm thinking.

Because we must look at the reason for Cecilia's fight and flight. For her stance and her resistance. We must look at the reason she chose martyrdom, why she embraced death rather than return to the Greco-Roman world of her father.

The answer lies in the second part of our story, in the origin of the word "virgin." The early church had a really marvelous, truly unique understanding of women. It was started by Jesus, of course. Just take one example. Take the story of the road to Emmaus. While the two disciples were walking along together, and Jesus asked them, they recounted the story of the passion: "and besides all this, it is now the third day since this took place. Some women from our group astounded us: they were at the tomb early in the morning."[1] Wait a minute, wait: "Women of our group"? Women were not allowed to study with rabbis at that time. I remember that movie *Yentl*, where the woman had to disguise herself as a young boy in order to study Torah in the *shul*. Even now, in Orthodox Judaism women are not allowed to study Torah with the rabbis. But Jesus allowed women in his group right

---

1. Luke 24:21–22.

alongside the men. Women and men, together as disciples of Jesus. Two thousand years ago. And whom did Jesus choose to be the "apostle of the resurrection"? No man; rather, Mary Magdalene, the apostle to the apostles.

The early church, with the power of the Holy Spirit strong amidst her, followed Christ's lead. Women were the heads of households and household churches. They were prophets and healers and deacons, according to the Scriptures. Researching another topic, I was looking through the documents of the Council of Nicaea, and at the very end were the "anathemas": banishment-type statements for people who held certain beliefs or engaged practices that were unacceptable for the Church. And the last three anathemas were about deaconesses. I forgot what they were for, but the point is that there were women deacons in the Catholic Church—even up to three hundred years after the resurrection.

Anyway, the early church stood out in comparison to the ambient Greco-Roman culture, and even the Jewish culture of the time. In the Roman world, for example, women could inherit, or even sue in court. But only if they were the daughter of . . . or the wife of . . . In other words, women had rights, but they were derivative ones: rights that were dependent on men, and came to them from their relationships to men. If, on the other hand, they had no men, as in the case of widows, they could be in pretty desperate situations.

But in its following Jesus through the inspiration of the Spirit, the early church was different. Women had roles and duties and rights in the early church, but they were not derivative from men: the status of every person came directly from their relationship to God in Christ. This was recognized and honored in the early church. Well, needless to say, the church had socially and culturally created an entirely new being. As it says in the Scripture: "So whoever is in Christ, there is a new creation."[2] And again, "There is no longer male and female; for all of you are one in Christ Jesus."[3] So now that there are a bunch of these new, independent beings in the new, Christ-following community, it's clear you can't call them by any of their old names. So they reached back into their heritage, and just as with the word *agape*, they found and baptized a word to describe this new woman in Christ. They called her *Parthenos*, a "virgin." Evidently, that's what that word meant in the early church: an independent woman who stood before God *as herself*. Just the person relying on God. It seemed, then, that it didn't

2. 2 Cor 5:17.
3. Gal 3:28.

make much difference whether you were married or not, or whether you had children. They called you a virgin to designate this independence you enjoyed in Christ in the new community.

In fact, Josephine Massyngbaerde Ford, who had extensively researched this phenomenon, told me that she found in the catacombs of Rome several dedications "to my virgin mother."[4] Because it wasn't so much about sex, this virgin thing. It was about a new kind of dignity and status for women, a new independence and reverence found in Christ and in his bride, the church. And while we're at it, that was why Mary was "the virgin of virgins." She could even have a *child* without a man—directly from within her relationship to God. What an example of virginity she was and is!

Well, as one might imagine, the men in the ambient culture just couldn't buy this revolutionary understanding of women. Some men are enraged to find that women are escaping their imagined control. A history professor colleague of mine told me that some men in our country poured boiling water down the throats of women suffragists. It was not so different in the empire of Rome. In the culture around the new faith community, fathers tried to arrange for marriages for their daughters, so that she, the daughter of . . . could have the added status of being the wife of . . .

But the Christian women, the virgins, resisted. Not because they didn't want to be married. Some of them were married and even had children in the Christian community. What they did not want was to return to derivative status or be defined by anyone other than God. They refused to become second-class citizens or surrender the freedom and special dignity they had found in the body of Christ, the church, his bride. "For freedom Christ has set us free," wrote Paul. "So stand firm and do not submit again to a yoke of slavery."[5]

Stand firm they did. They did not submit again. And they died, died in scores and maybe even in hundreds: Barbara, virgin and martyr; Christina, virgin and martyr; Alexandria, virgin and martyr; Columba of Sens, virgin and martyr; Apollonia of Alexandria, virgin and martyr; Lucy, virgin and martyr; Agatha, virgin and martyr; Felicity, virgin and martyr.

And yes, Cecilia, virgin and martyr.

---

4. The late Dr. Ford was a New Testament and rabbinic scholar at the University of Notre Dame. Simon knew her from his time as a doctoral student there.

5. Gal 5:1.

So, to come full circle, I find myself wondering, was it really such a mistake that Cecilia became the patroness of music? Maybe not.

Because I don't know about anyone else, but when I reflect upon why she died, about her freedom and her dignity and her independence and her courage to resist the forces of oppression and violence that wanted to take those Christ-given gifts away from her, when I reflect on her love of Christ and of her love of her life in him, and when I reflect on how she clung to that life even unto her death in this world . . . then all of a sudden, I find I feel like singing.

Philip's Reflection

Intrigued by Simon's meditation, I found discrepancies among online stories of Cecilia. According to the Franciscan website, she was married to Valerian, and executed by three strokes to the neck. The site also acknowledges that stories of her are legend,[6] and no other site mentioned those Latin mistranslations Simon pointed out. Are these historical discrepancies important in discovering where Jesus, faith, and discipleship are within her story? I will leave that to the reader and their prayerful contemplations. My commentary focuses on where my spirit was moved, and I invite readers to allow themselves to notice the movement of the Holy Spirit within themselves when reflecting on her martyrdom. Our receptivity allows us to apprehend truth(s), to see God revealed in all things, and as always, to deepen our relationship with Christ so that we could love and serve him more fully.

Saint Cecilia's Christian status, and martyrdom, reminds me that when we walk closely in the company of Jesus, we understand that he desires our freedom from all constraints. Examining Cecilia's cultural inequities and constraints helps us see current applications.

Cecilia's personal and social identity—her status—as a follower of Christ was stifled by her society's norms and practices. Transformed by her relationship with Jesus, she sacrificed everything in this life to stay faithful to that union. Early Christians' language failed to accommodate the entirety of new spiritual realities they experienced. Just as they had appropriated the word *agape* to attempt to capture the kind of love Christ illuminated,[7]

6. Franciscan Media, "Saint Cecilia."

7. See Krznaric, "Ancient Greeks," lines 1–101 for more information on Greek words for love. Simon discussed with me his understanding of the early followers' decision to

Simon teaches us that early Christians also appropriated the term *Parthenos*. Can we relate today's realities to Cecilia's struggles with her social and personal identities?

We too are bound by social definitions, cycles of socialization that lead us to stigmatize, dehumanize, and to judge negatively through automatic thinking and implicit biases. But Jesus humanizes and cherishes everyone, even those we are often "bound" to disdain. Our transformation may be helped by this prayer: If we want to glimpse the mind of Jesus, we should pray to see all others through his eyes, and to love them as he loves them. Perhaps another obstacle hindering us in that love are the times we lose our own felt-sense of God's love and embrace.

Christ's liberating graces are available to overcome all obstacles. My studies and interviews of people struggling under oppression often led me to deep feelings of sympathy, and sometimes despair, at their endless suffering. But therein also lies a trap that interferes with the fullness of his salvific graces. If I choose to *stay* in the wounded areas, even in compassion, I am likely to foment anger and frustration.[8] Those strong emotions are self-generating, fueled by my mind's inability to find comprehensive solutions. If I turn to listen, God reminds me that it is not my responsibility to analyze the mystery of human suffering successfully and completely. I want to be in partnership with God, certainly not the one in charge!

We Christians can choose to believe the good news that Jesus completed his salvific mission. At any moment, we can participate in the continual invitation to walk the liberating journey with Christ. Put another way, when we get caught up for too long in the graphic, real pain of Good Friday, we limit our receptivity to the ever-present hope and transcendence of Easter Sunday.

Questions to Consider: Provide specific instances of how Jesus treated the women he encountered. Recalling how women were seen by his ambient culture, what do his attitudes and actions mean for men and women today? Acknowledging Mary Magdalene as the "apostle of the resurrection,"

---

take *agape* from the several words Greek words for love, and repurpose it to approximate the love Jesus lived and expressed. It signified a selfless love of all; loving without the expectation or desire for reciprocation. *Agape* helps us understand Jesus' command to love our enemies. Not only are we not getting anything positive in return from them, as we would for the other kinds of love, like *eros* or *philia*, we are likely to get enmity instead.

8. See Matt 5:22. In that passage, Jesus expressly forbids us to foment anger, because it is an emotion that can quickly lead us away from the nonviolent kingdom.

discuss why her social identities are important to disciples today, as opposed to the ways those identities limited her in her culture. How specifically were the rights of women in the early church different from their rights in the Roman state, and in the Jewish culture? Beyond the obvious denotation of sexual relations, what did the term "virgin" connote in the early church? How could Cecilia's witness and martyrdom inspire us? How could Cecilia's life and martyrdom be viewed as a representation of how Jesus desires our freedom?

In God's kingdom on earth, as it is in heaven, our truest identity is not derived from any social, relational, or socioeconomic status; every person's status comes directly from their relationship to God in Christ.

19

Jesus' Call to His Beloved Cannot Be Silenced (2 Timothy 2:8–13)

The Roman martyrology records that for a period of forty years, fifty-five Jesuits suffered martyrdom during their missionary work in Japan. Through the little known, astonishing life of Christopher Ferreira—the final Jesuit martyr there—we are reminded that miracles happen when we are responsive to Jesus' loving, continual call to us. No sin is too large to be forgiven, and Jesus' steadfast and loving invitation to Christopher to return to him reminds us that we are never beyond the reach of his loving embrace. As Jesus was with Christopher, we are inspired to act patiently and persistently with those who sin against us or others.

Saint Paul Miki and Companions, Martyrs

I LOVE BEING THE center of attention. Like Mark Twain, at weddings I want to be the bride; at funerals I want to be the corpse. I think it's one of the reasons I like preaching at Mass or teaching in a classroom. As a result, I've always had a bit of a problem with memorials such as these. I mean, we always talk about Paul Miki and Companions, martyrs. Or Isaac Jogues and Companions, martyrs. Felicity, Perpetua, and Companions, martyrs.

I imagine what it might be like to be a martyr. I think about being a proud member of a courageous community of Jesuits, bravely facing threats of death because of our commitment to Jesus and the gospel. And maybe, finally, we would be found worthy of martyrdom together. I imagine that.

Regarding St. Paul Miki—and companions—I decided to look up one of the lives of one of the companions who died in Japan during the forty years that our brothers suffered martyrdom in the Japanese mission.

I remember the book and television series *Shogun*. When the shogun finally did take full power in Japan, he decided to do away with all Western influences, the principal of which was Christianity. If a person were charged with being a Christian, the imperial court would compel that person to apostatize. If the Christian would not, the court would subject him or her to horrifying tortures. They would crucify Christians, weigh them down under freezing rivers until they died, flay them alive, or cut them behind the ear and hang them upside down until they bled to death. Not only that, but the Christian's entire family would be ordered to be killed—whether or not they were Christians themselves. Anyone in the village who knew about but did not turn a Christian in would be sentenced to death—and his or her whole family, too.

Well, understandably, with the fear of torture and death, the Catholic community began to collapse under persecution, dying or denying the faith in large numbers. Back in Europe, the Jesuits went to a guy named Christopher Ferreira, who was then the provincial of Portugal.[1] They said, "Christopher, the Japanese mission is in trouble." And in the tradition of Jesuit missionaries, Christopher Ferreira said, "I'm your man." Within a few days he was on a ship to Japan.

During the eight-month journey, Ferreira learned Japanese well enough to communicate. When he got to Japan, he hit the ground running. He started secret catechism classes for the new Christians. He started secret seminaries for Japanese who wanted to serve as sacramental ministers. He went around celebrating secret Masses with the threatened Catholic communities, encouraging them to keep to the faith, even in the face of torture and death. And gradually, the Catholic community strengthened, even beginning to increase in numbers under his direction. In his own day and to his own face, Christopher Ferreira was called, "the savior of the Japanese mission."

But one day, Christopher was celebrating a secret Mass with about a hundred Japanese Catholics, hidden away in an upstairs room. The Japanese Imperial Forces discovered their hiding place, broke in, arrested all the Christians, and brought them to the imperial court. Of those hundred

---

1. The Society of Jesus was and is organized in provinces or geographic regions, each headed by a provincial superior appointed by the Superior General in Rome.

who were viciously tortured, only one apostatized. Imagine! Only one renounced the faith. Under the massive cruelty of torture, only one denied that Jesus was the Lord: Christopher Ferreira.

And that wasn't all. Never one to do anything halfway, Christopher turned to work as a translator for the Japanese imperial courts, trying to convince other Christians to apostatize as he had apostatized, and handing them over to torture and death if they would not. He did this work day after day for eighteen years.

Then one day, one day after those eighteen years, at the end of a trial that condemned yet another group of Christians to death, Christopher turned to the judge and said, "You're going to have to kill me, too. I'm a Christian."

So, they took him and they tortured him, tortured him with the same violence they had years earlier, but this time Ferreira would not relent, would not renounce the faith, would not deny that Jesus was his Lord. This time, violence did not win. This time, Christopher remained faithful unto death. The Roman martyrology says that we Jesuits suffered fifty-five martyrs, companions of Paul Miki, in the Japanese mission. Christopher Ferreira was the fifty-fifth.

I'm imagining how many times every day during those eighteen years that Christopher wandered away, how many times every day Jesus asked him, "Christopher, do you love me? Christopher Ferreira, do you love me?" until he finally heard, turned again, overcame his fear of violence and death, and followed his Master to the cross.

What am I to learn from Christopher Ferreira's apostasy—and his return? What does his story say to me? Well, I don't apostatize with a capital "A," the way Christopher did. But I tell you, I do apostatize with little "a's" all the time. I mean, Jesus is Lord, sure. But not over my relationship with this particular Jesuit. Jesus is Lord, yes, but not over this television remote. Jesus is Lord, okay, but I can figure out how to set up this Center for Peacemaking by myself. Lots of apostatizing—with little "a's."

Through all of this, Jesus always stays with me, calling me by name. As he always stayed with Christopher. As he always stays with us, his companions. Always. How are we to respond to this Jesus who, despite our too frequent wanderings, still gives and forgives so extravagantly? When we submit to our fear of death and become servants of violence, how are we companions to respond to such a Lord who, as we hear in the Scriptures, remains faithful always, even when we are unfaithful?

I think of the days of Christopher Ferreira, and the answer comes to me. It comes to me each morning when I read the Invitatory Psalm of the Office: "Oh, that today you would hear his voice: Harden not your hearts . . ."[2]

Philip's Reflection

Although they provide us with inspiring and courageous witness, we do not have to be saints to be loved by Christ, always. Christopher's story reveals important lessons for us. First, there is nothing one can do to extinguish God's eternal faithfulness, love, and mercy for each of us. Also, if we look deeply at ourselves, we may find ways in which we deny God's primacy in our lives. Recognizing those allows us to ask God for graces to participate more completely with God's will and to become more liberated. We also note that ordinary, unknown people provide extraordinary witness and discipleship. And finally, we must remember to keep our hearts open to receive God's omnipresent invitation to walk with us in all parts of life.

Christopher Ferreira's life provides me with a stunning reminder of God's steadfast faithfulness and mercy. Jesus redeems us from the darkness of humanity's heart, and heals the damage from violence, both from what we inflict, and what is inflicted on us. That violence can range from a depersonalizing slur, to institutionalized oppression, poverty, or one of the horrific forms of torture and murder like the Japanese used during their attempt to purge Christianity from their country. Jesus also redeems us from our own fears of diminishment, and ultimately from our natural weaknesses and physical death. As Jesus has continually demonstrated—such as forgiving his executioners from the cross, and forgiving Peter's abandonment—our God does not hold a grudge. Christopher's story reminds us that we cannot scare him away or cause him to stop inviting us, to stop his compassion and mercy, to stop him from loving us. My soul rejoices in Jesus' endless faithfulness in me, in us.

Yet I still felt a lingering darkness after reading Christopher's story. At first, I was deeply disturbed at the relentless cruelty of the persecutors and the terrible decisions the victims faced. I wanted to learn more about why the Japanese government officials did those things. Perhaps if I could understand it better, I could excuse it more easily. I researched more, but I remained dismayed. Clearly, the forces that seek to darken the Light of

2. Ps 95:8.

God, to create maximum fear and acquiescence, were heartily at work in Japan then. I tried to imagine the challenges to faith that the accused and their families faced. I knew that God provided powerful graces to each in order to face their ordeal.

Staying longer with my discomfort, I realized an important omission: I had not invited God to accompany me during my research. Reading of the torture and murder of the missioners and Japanese Christians hardened my heart to the persecutors. I noticed that my mind and heart were being co-opted in an insidious way that closed it to hearing God's voice. I was fooled into feeling, then thinking, that my deep sense of sympathy for the victims, coupled with my anger at the perpetrators, were sufficient evidence of my commitment to building the kingdom of God. Shortly after reading the third research article, I recalled that early in my Ignatian Spiritual Exercises, I was directed to pray imaginatively about how God sees the world. When I brought my sadness and dismay at those cruelties to God's vision, God helped lift my emotions. This maxim came to mind: "Never fight against evil as though it were entirely outside of yourself." I reflected on my own intolerances, my impulses at violence. God helped me to humbly open to God's limitless compassion, mercy, and forgiveness for all—killers and apostates. Since our Master forgave his killers, I must pray for the grace to forgive those, and all transgressors.

When I prayerfully reflect on how to apply the witness of the martyrs to discipleship today, I must avoid trivializing their sacrifice through weak application. A valid lesson is that we should continually turn first and always to what Jesus said and did to help us choose life-enriching actions. That seems especially pertinent when our personal interest and safety of ourselves and others is at stake. We also have an "ace" to always play: guidance through prayer to the Advocate Jesus left us.

Another valid, practical, and personal application of the martyrs' sacrifice is to examine the times we deny God's primacy; the "small a" of apostasy. Apostasy is defined in Webster's online dictionary as "an act of refusing to continue to follow, obey, or recognize a religious faith."[3] What are today's influential, powerful voices telling me to disobey Jesus, to choose resentment and enmity? Is one of my apostasies acting impatiently or speaking insultingly to those who disagree with my sense of discipleship? Can my apostasy even be doing peace and social justice work on my own, convincing myself I do not need to follow God's ways?

3. Merriam-Webster.com, s.v. "apostasy," line 1.

While honest self-examination is critically important,[4] we must also strive to do so in Jesus' company. If the fruits of my prayerful reflection yield only self-diminishment, as in, "I could never endure that torture of myself and my family; therefore, I am not a committed Christian"—then my heart cannot be as open as it need be to hear God's voice to me, now. I become an enemy to myself.

An enemy is anyone or any force that encourages me to feel or think less of myself; to stay in pain and suffering, and to despair and feel unconnected to God, myself, and others. Temptations to diminish myself originate in painful losses and life experiences. The evil spirit thrives in those places. Christopher Ferreira's life reminds us that no matter how long we have been "away" from Jesus, if we just listen, if we open our heart to allow for God's presence anywhere in creation, we will hear him. We are not God's enemy, and God is not our enemy. With God's graces, I can quickly identify the temptations to despair and separation, and open my heart more fully to receive God's ineffable love and mercy.

Questions to Consider: The 2016 film *Silence*, directed by Martin Scorsese, highlighted some of the trials suffered by the Jesuits under the forty-year persecution by the Japanese government. How did you react to those events, or the ones in Simon's reflection? Share a story of a martyr or one persecuted for their faith. What does "apostatize" mean to you and your faith practice? What action(s) could one take that would put them outside of God's forgiving love? Even if we are not called as disciples to be physically martyred, what aspects from the martyrs' courageous and faithful witness can we apply to our own faith, our own discipleship?

In the kingdom of God, even apostasy is forgiven when we wholeheartedly answer Jesus' loving call to repent and to return to him.

---

4. See O'Brien, *Ignatian*, 75–77, for the prayer of the Daily Examen in Ignatian Spiritual Exercises; see *Alcoholics Anonymous*, 85–88, for discussion of Step Eleven's daily self-examination.

Afterword

WE HOPE THAT READERS have experienced graces that have brought them closer to Jesus. We end by offering a prayer exercise designed to deepen any graces and insights.

Using Jesus' parable of the Sower, found within all the Synoptic Gospels, the following prayerful activity invites the reader to look back at parts of our book, introduce and apply Ignatius's three phases of spiritual growth, and look ahead to continue to nurture our relationship with God and confidently build God's kingdom.

After setting aside a period of uninterrupted time, notice your breathing, taking a few deep inhalations and exhalations. Become aware of God's sustaining presence in your breaths. Read the parable in each Gospel: Matthew 13:1–24, Mark 4:1–29, and Luke 8:4–18. Enter the scene, imagining as many sense details as you can. Picture the Sower scattering the seeds on various terrain. What was he wearing? Was he speaking or singing as he sowed the seeds? Who are you in the scene, and where are you? Is it warm, can you feel the sun? After a while, allowing the Spirit to move you, see Jesus explaining the parable to you. What metaphoric "soil and growing conditions" are you currently experiencing? Speak to him about which "soil" you desire to be, and ask for what you need from him.[1] You may wish to thank him for your current place, or your desire may be to move to more fertile soil to maximize your yield. Be sure to leave space for silent listening.

Ignatius's first phase of spiritual growth is developing a friendship with Jesus. Which readings in our book have helped you to develop that friendship? Return to and savor them often, asking for God to deepen that experience. Did chapter 6 remind you of God's call to you? You may ask of Jesus, What else do you want me to know or feel about that experience?

---

1. If we recognize that we do not have the desire, Ignatius advises us to pray for the desire, or for the desire for the desire, etc.

Repetition, and a return to a graced period, is an important practice in the Exercises, and in going forward in your journey with Jesus. Within this parable, the birds ate the trampled seed. We can expect resistance to our movement to friendship with Jesus. Ignatius believed that the evil spirit does not want us to believe in God, and to be saved. As pervasive and apparently powerful as the forces of evil are, God's power is stronger. Tom McMurray, SJ reminded me that when (not if!) tempted, to ask for God's grace to reject evil and to embrace God's way of seeing all of me.

Ignatius's second phase is allowing ourselves to be transformed by our relationship with Jesus. Recall chapters 1 and 2, and how Mary and Joseph each faced terrible cultural and intergenerational obstacles, but still chose to allow themselves to be transformed by their relationship with God. Returning to the parable of the Sower, determine if Jesus, the Word of God, has grown, but has not been tended or taken root in us. If not, why? Have we forgotten to speak regularly to him as our friend? Have we been ridiculed for our faith? Laughed at because of the "idealism" of Christ-like nonviolence and forgiveness? Consider returning to another chapter which dealt with trials and persecutions followers faced. How did they encounter Jesus during their testing? Share with Jesus how you felt when challenged, and ask him for what you need. When Christians, non-Christians, and atheists ridicule us for our belief, it may help to remember this: Saint Augustine wrote that "Unless you believe, you will not understand." And recall within the miraculous raising of Lazarus in chapter 13, Jesus told us, "If you believe, you will see the glory of God."[2] Remember our decision to believe is sometimes enough for Jesus to work with us. For followers of Jesus, believing is seeing ourselves and the world differently.

The third Ignatian spiritual phase is engaging with our ongoing conversion towards a prophetic stance. Webster's dictionary indicates that the word "prophet" comes from a Greek word meaning "speaking for."[3] Chapter 5 invites us to give the Christ-life within us our own words, spoken to the world. Nonviolence always seeks conversion, not coercion; to see a person's humanity, and not to reduce them to a label or object. What words will we unlearn and never speak as though it were of Christ—justified violence? War? Capital punishment? Apostasies? Which actions of ours give greater glory to God and the kingdom? Which actions are in opposition to that kingdom, more in line with kingdoms of this world? Even if we do

2. John 11:40.
3. *Merriam Webster's Collegiate Dictionary*, 11th ed. (2006), s.v. "prophet," 996.

transgress, like Peter, the Hindu man in chapter 11, and Christopher Ferreira in chapter 19, when we repent, Jesus will embrace us with mercy and forgiveness.

Jesus' parable assures us of obstacles to the word's growth. When the word grows amidst thorns, it takes hold for a while, but is choked off by worries, focusing only on this life and ourselves. We can expect that as the word "ripens" in us and begins to bear fruit, and we get closer to God, the evil spirit moves to take us away from that closeness. For the word to produce bountifully in us, we must reaffirm our purpose in life, articulated in the first key meditation in the Exercises: "I am created to praise, love, and serve God."[4]

We can ask God to open our hearts to continually discover God in wondrous and unexpected ways, to deepen our friendship, to give us the graces through the Holy Spirit to love everyone in the ways Jesus did, and to invite all to help us build his nonviolent kingdom.

Let us speak and act with conviction in the loving ways of the nonviolent Jesus, to whom "all power in heaven and on earth" has been given.[5] He has defeated evil and converted death, and promises to be "with us always, even until the end of the age."[6]

4. O'Brien, *Ignatian*, 63.
5. Matt 28:18.
6. Matt 28:20.

APPENDIX A

Best Practices Guidelines for Individual, Pair, or Group Study

I STRUCTURED THIS BOOK to be used for prayerful exploration by individuals and groups. I based the book's questions on established critical thinking and inquiry techniques. I grounded my group collaboration suggestions on six main sources: Questions my spiritual directors asked me during the Ignatian Exercises; my forty years of teaching, specifically in my leading collaborative, cooperative, and democratic class discussions; my design and facilitation of comprehensive and innovative professional development and learning programs for teachers and administrators; my doctoral graduate work, especially, researched-based best practices for intra- and intergroup dialogues; and revisions based on feedback from adult faith formation groups I facilitated, using this book's format.

Individual Exercise

I suggest setting aside a minimum of twenty uninterrupted minutes. Begin with prayer, asking for guidance from the Holy Spirit throughout.[1] Affirm that God desires a deep communion with each of us, and that by sitting and placing yourself in Jesus' company, you are answering his invitation to fully share your life with him. Select a chapter from our book, and choose an option below which feels most appropriate. A prayer from Saint Thomas More comes to mind: "[Creator God], you have given us a mind to know

1. Simon always advised me to pray to the Holy Spirit whenever I was pondering the Scriptures. His logic was convincing: speak with the author when seeking to understand the text's meaning.

you, a will to serve you, and a heart to love you. Be with us today in all that we do, so that your light may shine out in our lives." For any of the options, pay attention to your body, noticing any energy there. Remember to keep looking to God as you notice your breaths.

Option 1: To direct your focus, first read and answer the questions following your selected chapter. This helps you attend to main ideas, and alerts you to your thoughts and feelings. Read the scriptural passage (if applicable) and our two reflections. Return to your answers, and determine if your thoughts and feelings have been reinforced, changed, and if new questions have arisen for you.

Option 2: Read the entire book prior to addressing the questions. Return to answer the chapter questions and those in Appendix B. This strategy works well for those whose optimal learning style progresses from global to specific.

Option 3: All but three of Simon's meditations responded to a scriptural passage. First, read the pertinent New Testament passage to get an overview. Then, read the passage again, attending to salient details or images. Note your feelings; determine the person in the passage with whom you most closely identify. Be still as you picture the scene in as much sensory detail as you can, and notice your interior movement as it arises, without forcing anything.[2] Next, read Simon's meditation, and reflect again upon your thoughts and feelings. Was there anything he wrote that was like your imagined scene? Anything new or different? How might Jesus be communicating to you at this moment? Then, read my reflection. Did it provide a different lens to access any other thoughts and feelings? Take note of these within your heart and mind. I found it useful to keep some brief notes, though at times I would be moved to write a more extensive journal entry. End with a closing prayer.

The following questions and suggestions from my spiritual directors have general application for any option: What questions arise from the scriptural passage? Can you find the answers in the Scripture itself? How has God spoken to you in the past, and does that earlier communication apply now? If so, pray for a deepening of those prior graces. Search for Jesus in any circumstance of your life.

---

2. Ignatius also calls for a colloquy, which is an imagined conversation between you and someone in the scriptural scene. See footnote 3 in the Introduction for additional information.

Pair or Group Study

The second distinct examination can provide benefits inherent to effective collaborative learning with partners, small groups, classrooms, or faith groups. Whenever possible, bookend the discussion with a group prayer, or at minimum, a personal prayer, asking especially for the intercession of the Holy Spirit of Truth.

With a partner or small group, it is best to share faith experiences in a trusting environment. Many find sharing spiritual matters an intimate exchange, producing feelings of vulnerability. Establish discussion guidelines that help each feel safe in sharing, acknowledging that it can be affirming and sometimes challenging to share faith journeys. Regardless of others' reactions to your sharing, bring everything back to God in prayer for discernment.

Here are best practices tips for effective collaboration for larger groups: Determine if there is to be a group leader to help facilitate discussion. A group's efficacy is most often positively impacted by a skilled facilitator who helps keep focus, encourages equal participation, reflects to the group with limited personal judgment, and is not loquacious. While individuals have their own inclinations or training for facilitation, it helps for the leader to occasionally do a quick informal check-in with the group. Prompts like, "How is the pace so far?" or "Has everyone who wishes to share done so?" acknowledge that all are of equal importance, and that the group members can be a resource to each other. Many find it helpful if the facilitator ends the session by inviting each person to share a movement of the heart, mind, or spirit, or a planned action. That prompt helps to crystallize what can be ethereal discussions.

For groups that meet regularly, like classrooms or faith study groups, it is important to establish group norms. In classrooms, the main facilitator is the professor or teacher. If the class follows a democratic discussion format, the facilitator encourages a format whereby each viewpoint is equally valued, and students will rotate as discussion facilitators. Suggested guidelines include: establishing conditions that help each person feel safe for personal sharing, and address each person's learning style, at least sometimes. Agreements around confidentiality are important for safety and intragroup trust. Suggested wording for that agreement is that the person telling their story "owns their story," and that no one in the group can retell another person's story outside the group. The group's ideas can be shared if the person's identity is kept private. Members should check with adherence to their guidelines, and modify as necessary.

People are in different places in their faith journeys, and have different comfort levels in sharing. Especially for faith groups, I suggest that the group initially determines its goals. Does the group wish to argue the pros and cons of important issues like Just War Theory, abortion, perceived misogyny in the Catholic Church, female ordination in the Catholic Church? Effective group function includes presenting and adhering to an open agenda; clearly stated purposes; respect for boundaries (including following start and stop times); equitable use of talk time; and incorporation of silence within discussion periods, since most need time to individually process. I highly recommend incorporating quiet reflective time, which can include a directed question or self-directed writing. Let participants know if they will be asked to share their writing, and honor refusals. Respect boundaries and safety by alerting participants prior to their reflective writing if they would be asked to share their writing with others. Breakout groups are helpful, and those reporting back from the small to larger group should always get permission to share, since many share more comfortably in smaller settings. During discussions, participants may choose silence, but should never be silenced by others in the group. For those who do not like to speak extemporaneously, reading a part of their reflection or commenting on another's sharing helps add their voice, and aids the group's collaborative function.

Our book often raised and challenged commonly held beliefs, including challenging the accuracy of "common sense," which is sometimes used to justify an inequitable, exclusionary status quo. An essential practice of social justice education is identifying individuals or groups whose voices are absent, muted, or misrepresented, and seeking their actual voices, or imagining how the story or topic would be different if they were authentically included. We have repeatedly noticed that Jesus invites everyone into the kingdom.

As we get to know Jesus more closely, and engage with his compassion, love, and forgiveness, we can use our individual and collective creativity to enact his nonviolent love in all group discussions. As we have shown in our book, Jesus is eminently practical! While there will not always be universal agreement in a group discussion, sometimes hearing our own opinion aloud, or hearing the alternative viewpoints, helps us clarify or expand our own position. But we must not be afraid to try on new viewpoints, or to reconsider scriptural or commonly held interpretations.

Disagreements are bound to happen, especially for groups that meet over time. In fact, we can come to greater closeness and understanding by effectively working through them. Decide how the group will deal with conflicts and strong disagreements before they arise. Research indicates that the best way to talk across our differences is by focusing on our own experiences and beliefs, and not acting as a spokesperson for an ideology, a gender, a social status, etc. Also, we should speak about the issue, respect the other person's viewpoint, and never attack a person. Participants should be encouraged to notice when they are "triggered" by another person's viewpoint, and to try first to understand before responding from an emotionally charged place. A helpful technique is to have the responder accurately paraphrase the previous speaker's communication prior to adding their own.

Healthy group dynamics are fostered by occasionally doing a group function assessment. Do a clinical "fly on the wall" exercise, focusing on observed behaviors. In summary, I highly suggest that the group act in ways that are consistent with the nonviolent ways of Jesus. But let us also acknowledge that like us, Jesus also was a human with strong emotions!

Contemplative Listening and Dialoguing[3]

I thank my friend, Jane Morrissey, SSJ, for introducing this different collaborative activity to our local Pax Christi prayer group. I will illustrate this technique by delineating the steps I took when I facilitated our group's discussion of chapter 19.

The goal of the exercise is to foster the pair or group's collaborative creation. Picture the metaphor of the group filling a cup with its sharing. Prior to my facilitation, I prayed and considered several images associated with the persecuted Japanese Christians and Christopher Ferreira. I selected the resurrected Jesus entering the locked room of fearful disciples,[4] and began our meeting by offering it to the group as our focal image. I provided a minute or so of quiet reflection on that image, and asked if anyone

3. See Leadership Conference of Women Religious, "Contemplative Dialogue." The site includes a one-hour instructional video, complete with PDF files of the transcript, questions, goals, and more.

4. John 20:19.

wished to share from their reflection. I read Saint John's passage, and asked for two minutes of silent meditation on that scene, focusing on the sensory images. I asked if any images, senses, or words came to mind from their own memory or most recent experience. I invited each to speak, but no one could talk again until all others had a chance to speak. We were not to comment directly on what was previously spoken, sharing only what one felt moved to share in filling the communal cup. I then asked, How deep is Jesus' love for us individually and collectively? After another round of silence, participants shared their answers, some of which were images, songs, or other artist expressions. I listened for a common thread to the sharing, and noted it aloud.

Before I read Simon's "Saint Paul Miki and Companions, Martyrs," I asked them to listen to his meditation with their mind and heart, and note anything which addressed the question about the depth of Jesus' love, and the common thread I just noted. After reading, we sat in silence for five minutes. Individuals then shared, and I listened especially for commonalities, and selected an image, thought, or question that filled the metaphoric cup. I highlighted the commonalities, then asked what united us in hearing the word of God. I read my reflection in chapter 19. After a final round of silence, I asked them to share another image, thought, or question to add to the cup. I ended the activity by asking them to select, then share, one word, image, or grace that we could carry forth. We closed by praying the Lord's Prayer communally.

APPENDIX B

Final Review and Application Questions

WE CAN APPLY ELEMENTS of critical thinking skills to our spiritual life, since our mind, body, and spirit are connected. We continually refine the practice of our faith when we thoughtfully engage our mind and emotions, and revise as warranted.

As with all our activities, I encourage readers to start with prayer. Acknowledge God's presence in our life at this moment, and invite God into our hearts and minds as completely as we can. I often pray for special intercession from the Holy Spirit, our ultimate advocate; the power and truth that brought such profound insights to biblical people and writers, and who brought Jesus into this world and raised him from his violent murder.

The first general exercise is to review your journal, if you used one. If not, recall when you felt moved by something in the Scriptures, the reflections, or questions. Consider these questions:

1. Concerning your beliefs and faith prior to reading this book, what were you certain about? How has your certainty been supported?

2. Have your beliefs, or faith, been challenged? What has been the result?

3. Have you experienced new ideas or movements of your spirit? How do those feel to you today? Have you returned to them? If so, what have been the results? If not, why? Is that something you intend to do?

4. Identify and explain any new ways you have discovered to interpret the Scriptures.

5. Have you identified obstacles in deepening your journey with Jesus? If so, what are they, and are they internal or external? Can a Christian

community help with any of them, and how could it help you? Can you help someone with their obstacles? Have you brought your and others' obstacles to God?

6. What do you most desire in your relationship with God? What nurtures your relationship with God? Return to chapters, or other favorite scriptural readings, that deepened your personal relationship with Jesus, and savor the graces.

7. If you have discussed any parts of the book with another or others, how has the collaboration affected your thinking and feeling, your sense of connection to others, etc.?

8. Throughout this book, we considered the important issue of whether Jesus lived and taught an ethic of nonviolence, or justified violence, as seen in the various Christian church's official adoption of warfare for the past seventeen centuries. What are your thoughts and feelings about violence and its place in building earthly kingdoms and God's kingdom? What is your response to Pope Francis's call for all to "make active nonviolence our way of life"?[1]

9. How, specifically and practically, can *you* help build God's kingdom on earth, as it is in heaven?

10. Going forward, what will you do to participate with, to stay open to, God's love and grace?

1. Francis, "Nonviolence," 1.

Bibliography

"Acclamations in the Eucharistic Prayer." http://www.oremus.org/liturgy/tcw/ep-jan98/accl.html.

Adams, David. "The Seville Statement on Violence: A Progress Report." *Journal of Peace Research* 26.2 (1989) 113–21. http://www.jstor.org/stable/423863.

Albert Einstein Institution. https://www.aeinstein.org/.

Alcoholics Anonymous: The Story of How Many Thousands of Men and Women Have Recovered from Alcoholism. 3rd ed. New York: Alcoholics Anonymous World Services, 1976.

"The American Religious Landscape in 2020." *PRRI*, July 8, 2021. https://www.prri.org/research/2020-census-of-american-religion/.

Anonymous. "How Can I Keep from Singing?" Hymnary.org. https://hymnary.org/text/my_life_flows_on_in_endless_song.

Au, Wilkie, and Noreen Cannon Au. *God's Unconditional Love: Healing Our Shame.* New York: Paulist, 2016.

Benedict XVI, Pope. "Angelus." https://www.vatican.va/content/benedict-xvi/en/angelus/2007/documents/hf_ben-xvi_ang_20070218.html.

Bombay Sarvodaya Mandal and Gandhi Research Foundation. "Means and Ends." Comprehensive website by Gandhian Institutions, Bombay Sarvodaya Mandal and Gandhi Research Foundation. https://www.mkgandhi.org/voiceoftruth/meansandends.htm.

Brackley, Dean, SJ. "Remembering the Jesuit Martyrs of El Salvador: Twenty Years On." *Thinking Faith*, November 16, 2009. https://www.thinkingfaith.org/articles/20091116_1.htm.

Bucholz, Katharina. "The Top Ten Percent Own Seventy Percent of US Wealth." Statistica. https://www.statista.com/chart/19635/wealth-distribution-percentiles-in-the-us/.

Carlson, Peter. "The Crusader." *Washington Post*, December 15, 2002. https://www.washingtonpost.com/archive/lifestyle/2002/12/15/the-crusader/9de49dd7-43fd-45e0-a4ef-3df4475cb4a0/.

The Catholic Study Bible. New American Bible. New York: Oxford University Press, 1990.

Center for Christian Nonviolence. https://www.emmanuelcharlesmccarthy.org/.

Christian Community Bible. 49th ed. Quezon City, Philippines: Claretian, 2010.

Cruden, Alexander. *Cruden's Concordance.* Westwood, NJ: Barbour, 1987.

"The Difference between Patriotism and Nationalism." Merriam-Webster.com. https://www.merriam-webster.com/words-at-play/patriotism-vs-nationalism.

"Ever Ancient, Ever New: The Art and Practice of Lectio Divina." United States Conference of Catholic Bishops. https://www.usccb.org/bible/national-bible-week/upload/lectio-divina.pdf.

Francis, Pope. *Fratelli Tutti: On Fraternity and Social Friendship.* Huntington, IN: Our Sunday Visitor, 2020. Digital file.

————. *Laudato Si': On Care for Our Common Home.* https://www.vatican.va/content/francesco/en/encyclicals/documents/papa-francesco_20150524_enciclica-laudato-si.pdf.

————. "Nonviolence: A Style of Politics for Peace." https://www.vatican.va/content/francesco/en/messages/peace/documents/papa-francesco_20161208_messaggio-l-giornata-mondiale-pace-2017.html.

————. "Peace Memorial (Hiroshima)." https://www.vatican.va/content/francesco/en/messages/pont-messages/2019/documents/papa-francesco_20191124_messaggio-incontropace-hiroshima.html.

Franciscan Media. "Saint of the Day: Saint Cecilia." https://www.franciscanmedia.org/saint-of-the-day/saint-cecilia.

Ganss, George E., SJ. *The Spiritual Exercises of Saint Ignatius: A Translation and Commentary.* Chicago: Loyola, 1992.

Geneva International Centre for Justice. "Razing the Truth About Sanctions Against Iraq." https://www.gicj.org/positions-opinons/gicj-positions-and-opinions/1188-razing-the-truth-about-sanctions-against-iraq#:~:text=Around%201%2C500%2C000%20Iraqis%2C%20primarily%20children,which%20the%20country%20was%20left.

Harak, G. Simon, SJ. *Virtuous Passions: The Formation of Christian Character.* New York: Paulist, 1993.

Harak, G. Simon, SJ, ed. *Aquinas and Empowerment: Classical Ethics for Ordinary Lives.* Washington, DC: Georgetown University Press, 1996.

————. *Nonviolence for the Third Millennium: Its Legacy and Future.* Macon, GA: Mercer University Press, 2000.

Harak, Philip J. "Nonviolence in the Schools." In *Nonviolence for the Third Millennium: Its Legacy and Future,* edited by G. Simon Harak, SJ, 183–89. Macon, GA: Mercer University Press, 2000.

————. "Supporting Public High School Teachers in a Context of Multiple Mandates: A Social Justice Approach to Professional Learning Communities." EdD diss., University of Massachusetts, 2012. https://citeseerx.ist.psu.edu/viewdoc/download?doi=10.1.1.948.4857&rep=rep1&type=pdf.

————. "Remembering G. Simon Harak—A Powerful Ally of All Victims of War." *Waging Nonviolence,* November 30, 2019. https://wagingnonviolence.org/2019/11/remembering-simon-harak-powerful-ally-all-victims-war/.

The Holy See. "Nuclear Disarmament: Time for Abolition." Nuclear Age Peace Foundation. https://www.wagingpeace.org/nuclear-disarmament-time-for-abolition/.

International Campaign to Abolish Nuclear Weapons. https://www.icanw.org/.

International Committee of the Red Cross. https://www.icrc.org/en.

Jackson, Shirley. "The Lottery." *The New Yorker,* June 26, 1948. https://www.newyorker.com/magazine/1948/06/26/the-lottery.

Jesuits.org. https://www.jesuits.org/.

Just, Felix, SJ, ed. "Basic Texts for the Roman Catholic Eucharist: Eucharistic Prayers I–IV." Catholic Resources for Bible, Liturgy, Art, and Theology. https://catholic-resources.org/ChurchDocs/EP1-4.htm.

King, Martin Luther, Jr. *Strength to Love.* Philadelphia: Fortress, 1981.

Kizer, Kenneth W., and Suzanne Le Menestrel. *Strengthening the Military Family Readiness System for a Changing American Society.* Washington, DC: National Academies, 2019.

Krznaric, Roman. "The Ancient Greeks' 6 Words for Love (And Why Knowing Them Can Change Your Life)." *Yes Magazine,* December 28, 2013. https://www.yesmagazine. org/health-happiness/2013/12/28/the-ancient-greeks-6-words-for-love-and-why-knowing-them-can-change-your-life.

Ladinsky, Daniel, ed. *Love Poems from God: Twelve Sacred Voices from the East and West.* New York: Penguin, 2014. Digital file.

Leadership Conference of Women Religious. "Contemplative Dialogue." https://lcwr.org/ resources/contemplative-engagement/contemplative-dialogue.

Leonhardt, Douglas J., SJ. "Praying with Scripture." Ignatian Spirituality. https://www. ignatianspirituality.com/ignatian-prayer/the-what-how-why-of-prayer/praying-with-scripture/.

Maguire, Mairead. "Non-Violence and the Lost Message of Jesus." Inter Press Service News Agency. http://www.ipsnews.net/2014/12/opinion-non-violence-and-the-lost-message-of-jesus/.

Marquette University Center for Peacemaking. https://www.marquette.edu/peacemaking/.

McCarthy, Emmanuel Charles. "Behold the Lamb." Center for Christian Nonviolence. https://www.emmanuelcharlesmccarthy.org/retreats/.

———. *Christian Just War Theory: The Logic of Deceit.* Center for Christian Nonviolence. https://www.emmanuelcharlesmccarthy.org/category/booklets/.

Mecklin, John, ed. "At doom's doorstep: It is 100 seconds to midnight." 2022 Doomsday Clock Statement. Bulletin of the Atomic Scientists. https://thebulletin.org/ doomsday-clock/current-time/.

O'Brien, Kevin F., SJ. *The Ignatian Adventure: Experiencing the Spiritual Exercises of Saint Ignatius in Daily Life.* Chicago: Loyola, 2011.

Pasternak, Judith. "Another Death in the Family: Simon Harak, 1948–2019." War Resisters League. https://www.warresisters.org/another-death-family-simon-harak-1948-2019.

Pray As You Go. https://pray-as-you-go.org/.

Rohr, Richard. *Breathing under Water: Spirituality and the Twelve Steps.* Cincinnati: St. Anthony Messenger, 2011.

Shakespeare, William. *Complete Works.* New York: Harcourt, Brace & World, 1968.

Skehan, James William. *Place Me with Your Son: Ignatian Spirituality in Everyday Life.* Washington, DC: Georgetown University Press, 1991.

Steinhauer, Jennifer. "Suicides among Post-9/11 Veterans Are Four Times as High as Combat Deaths, a New Study Finds." *The New York Times,* October 22, 2021. https:// www.nytimes.com/2021/06/22/us/911-suicide-rate-veterans.html.

Treaty on the Prohibition of Nuclear Weapons. https://www.un.org/disarmament/wmd/ nuclear/tpnw/.

Twain, Mark. "The War Prayer." The American Yawp Reader. https://www.americanyawp. com/reader/19-american-empire/mark-twain-the-war-prayer-ca-1904-5/.

USA East Province of the Society of Jesus. Office of Ignatian Spirituality. https:// jesuitseastois.org/.

Voltaire Quotes. https://www.goodreads.com/quotes/108491-perfect-is-the-enemy-of-good.

Werfel, Franz. *The Song of Bernadette.* New ed. Translated by Ludwig Lewisohn. San Francisco: Ignatius, 2006.

Wester, John C. "Living in the Light of Christ's Peace: A Conversation Toward Nuclear Disarmament." https://archdiosf.org/documents/2022/1/220111_ABW_Pastoral_Letter_LivingintheLightofChristsPeace_Official_Reduced.pdf.

Winfield, Nicole. "Pope Francis Reaffirms Primacy of Conscience amid Criticism of 'Amoris Laetitia.'" *America: The Jesuit Review,* November 11, 2017. https://www.americamagazine.org/faith/2017/11/11/pope-francis-reaffirms-primacy-conscience-amid-criticism-amoris-laetitia.

Wink, Walter. *Jesus and Nonviolence: A Third Way.* Minneapolis: Fortress, 2003.

World Population Review. "Incarceration Rates by Country 2021." https://worldpopulationreview.com/country-rankings/incarceration-rates-by-country.